HD9397.972.C6 BIL

BOTTLED FOR BUSINESS

MAIN LIBRARY
QUEEN MARY, UNIVERSITY OF LONDON
Mile End Road, London E1 4NS
DATE DUE FOR RETURN

CANCELLED

NEW ACCESSIONS

2 7 FEB 2009

WITHDRAWN
FROM STOCK
QMUL LIBRARY

BOTTLED FOR BUSINESS

KARAN BILIMORIA

The less gassy guide to entrepreneurship

CAPSTONE

BICENTENNIAL

1807

WILEY

2007

BICENTENNIAL

Copyright © 2007 by Karan Bilimoria

First published 2007 by Capstone Publishing Ltd. (a Wiley Company)
The Atrium, Southern Gate, Chichester, PO19 8SQ, UK.
www.wileyeurope.com
Email (for orders and customer service enquires): cs-books@wiley.co.uk

The right of Karan Bilimoria to be identified as the author of this book has been asserted in accordance with the Copyright, Designs and Patents Act 1988

All Rights Reserved. No part of this publication may be reproduced, stored in a retrieval system or transmitted in any form or by any means, electronic, mechanical, photocopying, recording, scanning or otherwise, except under the terms of the Copyright, Designs and Patents Act 1988 or under the terms of a licence issued by the Copyright Licensing Agency Ltd, 90 Tottenham Court Road, London W1T 4LP, UK, without the permission in writing of the Publisher. Requests to the Publisher should be addressed to the Permissions Department, John Wiley & Sons Ltd, The Atrium, Southern Gate, Chichester, West Sussex PO19 8SQ, England, or emailed to permreq@wiley.co.uk, or faxed to (+44) 1243 770571.

Designations used by companies to distinguish their products are often claimed as trademarks. All brand names and product names used in this book are trade names, service marks, trademarks or registered trademarks of their respective owners. The Publisher is not associated with any product or vendor mentioned in this book. This publication is designed to provide accurate and authoritative information in regard to the subject matter covered. It is sold on the understanding that the Publisher is not engaged in rendering professional services. If professional advice or other expert assistance is required, the services of a competent professional should be sought.

Other Wiley Editorial Offices
John Wiley & Sons Inc., 111 River Street, Hoboken, NJ 07030, USA
Jossey-Bass, 989 Market Street, San Francisco, CA 94103–1741, USA
Wiley-VCH Verlag GmbH, Boschstr. 12, D-69469 Weinheim, Germany
John Wiley & Sons Australia Ltd, 42 McDougall Street, Milton, Queensland 4064, Australia
John Wiley & Sons (Asia) Pte Ltd, 2 Clementi Loop #02–01, Jin Xing Distripark, Singapore 129809
John Wiley & Sons Canada Ltd, 22 Worcester Road, Etobicoke, Ontario, Canada M9W 1L1
Wiley also publishes its books in a variety of electronic formats. Some content that appears in print may not be available in electronic books.

A catalogue record for this book is available from the British Library and the Library of Congress.

ISBN 13: 978-1-84112-726-2

Designed by Cylinder (www.cylindermedia.com)
Anniversary Logo Design: Richard J. Pacifico
Set in Stone by Sparks (www.sparks.co.uk)
Printed and bound in Great Britain by TJ International Ltd, Padstow, Cornwall

QM LIBRARY
(MILE END)

This book is printed on acid-free paper responsibly manufactured from sustainable forestry in which at least two trees are planted for each one used for paper production. Substantial discounts on bulk quantities of Capstone Books are available to corporations, professional associations and other organizations. For details telephone John Wiley & Sons on (+44) 1243–770441, fax (+44) 1243 770571 or email corporatedevelopment@wiley.co.uk

Dedication

I wish to dedicate this book to my father, Lt General Faridoon Bilimoria, who taught me more about life and leadership than could be contained in any number of pages. This is but a humble tribute to a man who gave me so much. I will forever be grateful to him.

CONTENTS

ACKNOWLEDGEMENTS

There can be no book without a story, and the Cobra story has been many years in the making. Through it all, we have enjoyed the support of so many people that the task of thanking them would fill a book in its own right. I can only say that Cobra's success is in the very fullest sense a team effort, and I am truly grateful for the assistance and encouragement of the team at Cobra Beer, the Indian restaurant industry, our stockists, distributors, suppliers, advisors and friends. Our journey together has been in every way a privilege.

Now that the story has become a book, I find myself in the debt of many others as well. First and foremost I must thank Steve Coomber, whose talents and patience brought the Cobra story to life, and Dominic Midgley, who wrote the foundation of the book. John Moseley, Julia Lampam, Iain Campbell, Grace O'Byrne, Kate Stanley and the rest of the team at Capstone have guided *Bottled for Business* from brainstorm to bookshelf. Although this is my first (and hopefully not last) book, I can say with confidence that one could wish for no more from a publisher.

I would also like to thank my wonderful wife, Heather. This book must ultimately be for my family, to whom the greatest debt is owed. They are, and have always been, unfailing in their support.

DIFFERENT, BETTER, CHANGING THE MARKETPLACE FOREVER

When someone makes a decision, he is really diving into a strong current that will carry him to places he had never dreamed of when he first made the decision.

From *The Alchemist* by Paulo Coelho

I n 2006 Cobra Beer's retail sales were £96m on sales in more than 45 countries. Over 100 people work out of the company's headquarters in London, and there are offices in New York, India and South Africa. Having won the Monde Selection Gold Award for quality, several years in succession, Cobra could justifiably claim to sell the best lager beer in the world. Yet, just 17 years ago, Cobra Beer was one man – Karan Bilimoria – and an idea.

This book is about Karan Bilimoria's business journey; from a half-formed idea to a global drinks business. It is about how a man, who was dismissed as 'not very creative', came to be running a £110m business empire founded on innovation. But more than that, it is a series of inspirational lessons, for anyone who hopes to run a business, who is running a business, or who works for a business. Like many entrepreneurs, Bilimoria has a distinctive business philosophy, a series of business principles that have served him well during his career. Some are born out of a deep seated personal conviction about the way things should be done. Some are things that he has learnt the hard way through trial and error. Some are things others have taught him. They are all here in the pages of this book.

CHAPTER ONE

PERSISTENCE PAYS

The tragedy of life doesn't lie in not reaching your goal. The tragedy lies in having no goal to reach. It isn't a disgrace not to reach the stars, but it is a disgrace to have no stars to reach for. It isn't a calamity to die with dreams unfulfilled, but it is a calamity not to dream.
Benjamin E. Mays, early 20th century American pastor and educator

IT STARTS WITH AN IDEA

Karan Bilimoria and beer go back a long way. Bilimoria grew up in India, where his father was an officer in the army, and it was there that he acquired a taste for the stuff. 'From the time I was allowed to drink, I've loved beer, absolutely loved it,' he says, 'I remember, for example, when I'd be with the young officers having a drink in one of the Indian Army messes, my father would walk past and ask "What's the young man drinking?" and they'd say, "Beer, Sir", and my father would say "Ah, good". In those days in India, people were brought up drinking whisky, but I always took a great liking to beer.'

When Bilimoria travelled to the UK in 1981, to continue his accountancy studies, his love of beer continued. As a student, money was tight. Home was the Indian YMCA on Fitzroy Square in London. For someone who could not cook it was a great location; the YMCA was surrounded by Indian restaurants and pubs, and Bilimoria would eat out at least twice a week.

It was at the Indian restaurants that Bilimoria discovered European lager. He was not impressed with the various lagers on offer, taking an instant dislike to them. 'I found them very gassy, very fizzy, very bland, very harsh and very bloating. Basically, they were difficult to drink.' Lager beer may have been the UK curry lover's drink of choice, but Bilimoria felt it was far from the most suitable.

'On the face of it, it made sense, because with the hot and spicy food, you feel like something cold and refreshing to go with it. Lager is meant to fit the bill. The problem was, especially with Indian food, that the combination of the fizzy lager and the spicy food bloated you up making it quite an unpleasant experience. I couldn't eat or drink as much as I wanted to. It was obvious that there was a business opportunity here: the restaurant owner could be selling me more food and more beer.'

Bilimoria considered the possibility that a pint of bitter and a vindaloo might make a better match. As a real ale fan he enjoyed a pint whether it was Fuller's London Pride or Charles Well's Bombardier. But, as a real ale fan he also knew that the combination of traditional beer and Indian food was not a good one. The ale was too heavy, too bitter and just didn't accompany the Indian food well. At the time, England, like the rest of the UK, was predominately an ale-drinking nation. Lager had made little impact on drinking habits. Rather than be downcast at the drinking habits of a nation, Bilimoria saw an opportunity. If the vast majority of beer consumed in the UK was of the real ale type, figured Bilimoria, then there must be a lot of other dissatisfied drinkers in Indian restaurants.

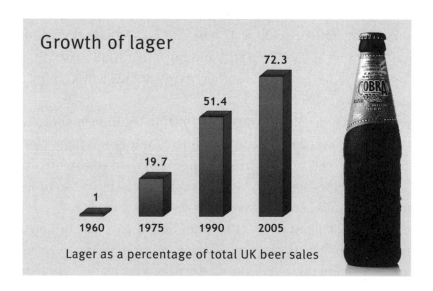

Growth of lager

72.3
51.4
19.7
1

1960 1975 1990 2005

Lager as a percentage of total UK beer sales

LAGER VS. ALE

For those wondering what the difference between a lager beer and a bitter beer, or ale, is: a lager is usually made using yeast which works at the bottom of the vat in cold temperatures (followed by a period for cool storage); ale is made using yeast that acts at the top of the vat in warmer conditions.

Work soon replaced study, but Bilimoria's sense that there was a business opportunity being missed continued to nag away at him. On his two-month-long trips to India to see his family (he had very accommodating employers who allowed him to save up overtime and take time off instead of extra pay), he would travel around the country, depending on where his father was posted, and sample local beers. 'I would drink all Indian brands,' he says. 'Depending on which part of the country I was in, I would drink Kingfisher, Rosy, Pelican, or – in the Indian army messes – Pals, Golden Eagle, or Black Label.' The locally-brewed beers were noticeably less gassy and smoother than their British counterparts.

It was on a visit to see his father – who retired as Commander-in-Chief of the Central India Army and at the time was a senior general commanding a corps stationed in North West India – that his rumination turned into resolve. Bilimoria, by now studying law at Cambridge, vividly recalls the day he and his father visited a brigadier friend, at a beautiful house in the hills at Simla, complete with wooden terrace overlooking the forest canopy in the valley below. 'I was looking out into the forest and drinking a beer at lunchtime,' he recalls. 'I just didn't enjoy drinking lagers in England. I said to myself, "I'm definitely going to do this. One day I'm going to take my own lager beer from here to England. It is going to be less gassy and smoother. It will accompany Indian food and it will appeal to ale drinkers." That moment I remember very clearly.'

WHAT DOES IT TAKE TO BE A SUCCESSFUL ENTREPRENEUR?

Thousands of people have good ideas, but how many of those ideas are ever translated into a business? Not many. The key is the entrepreneur. A good

KARAN'S BUSINESS TIPS:
DOING IT DIFFERENTLY

'It is tough coming up with a business idea that no one has ever thought of before. The good news for entrepreneurs is that you don't have to. Not quite, anyway. Because the innovation is not just important at the "What?" stage; it is equally important – if not more so – at the "How?" stage.

'Going into a competitive market, and the UK is the most competitive beer market in the world, with hundreds and hundreds of beer brands from all over the world available here, it would be easy to take the attitude, "it's so competitive what is the point of even starting?"' says Bilimoria. 'But I believe, however competitive a market is, however saturated it may appear to be, you can always start a brand, introduce a new product, by doing things differently in some way, by doing things better in some way, and in that way, changing the marketplace which you are going into forever.'

entrepreneur will find the right idea, maybe not the first time, and then find the resources to take that idea and build a business from it. The question then is, and it is one that has been asked countless times: What makes a good entrepreneur?

Different people have different takes on this thorny issue. Business academics will tell you that, even if you can't teach a person to be entrepreneurial, you can equip them with the skills they need to successfully start, run and grow a business. But that's not really an answer. Bilimoria, on the other hand, has a very clear idea of the qualities required to create a successful business; the qualities that have enable him to start his venture and take it all the way through to the £110m business it is today.

The ability to be creative

The first thing Bilimoria singles out is the ability to be creative. If your heart sinks when you read this, then you may be heartened to know that being creative does not necessarily equate with being good at art at school. Creativity is something that many people do not even realise they possess.

The brain contains between 10 to 100 billion neurons, each with hundreds of connections to adjacent neurons. Some people's neurons connect in a way that creates unusual, original, innovative ideas. Some people can encourage their brains to do this. To a degree, creativity is something that can be worked on and improved. There are techniques you can use, as Bilimoria does, which are detailed elsewhere in the Cobra story.

Throughout much of his childhood people told Bilimoria that he was not a creative person. Why? Because he was good at history, maths and science, but a useless artist. Therefore he was not creative. But they were wrong. Later in his life he discovered, through his first efforts to start a business, that one of his biggest advantages was his creativity.

'It is very important to think about creativity not as an isolated activity done in some kind of creativity silo,' says Bilimoria. 'It is a not a question of, "Right, I'm going to be creative now." Instead, strange as it may sound, it is a way of life. It is about being constantly engaged in everything you are doing. All the time try to think of original and new and different ways of doing and approaching things, driven by the knowledge that if you tackle life in this way you can add value and make a difference.'

Going the extra mile

Entrepreneurs must always go that one step further, says Bilimoria. You are not just going to do things because they have been done a certain way; you never accept things just because this is the way they are done. You are always trying to see if it can be done better in some way, or if you can take things further.

Bilimoria's recent appointment to the House of Lords is a good example of this constant boundary pushing. Most people would take the bureaucratic procedures of the Lords as set in stone, and not to be tampered with. Not Bilimoria.

Everyone who enters the House of Lords is required to make a maiden speech. It is a daunting moment, even for seasoned politicians. Sensibly, Bilimoria decided to prepare by reading previous maiden speeches recorded in *Hansard*, the edited verbatim report of proceedings in the House. The problem was that *Hansard* didn't distinguish the maiden speeches from any other speech.

'I asked why not,' says Bilimoria. Bemused staff replied that it had just never been done. 'I said, "well come on, can't we do it?" Hopefully now, Hansard might mark maiden speeches and hopefully it will be easier for future Lords to prepare for their maiden speech.'

Self-confidence and a great team

As an entrepreneur you must have confidence in your own abilities, as well as the abilities of others. So you need the ability to build a team around you. By 'team' Bilimoria does not only mean internal teams within the company, but also a team of external advisors, who believe in your ideas and are all willing to go that extra mile for you, whether they are your lawyers, accountants, advertising agency or factoring agency.

Become lucky

Successful business owners may appear lucky, but to a great extent, Bilimoria believes, they make their own luck. 'There is an element of luck, no question about it, but you make your own luck as well –you have got to be out there looking for the luck,' he says. 'Things aren't going to fall into your lap.'

If you look at the way the Cobra story pans out: getting into the market when an increasingly multicultural UK was willing to experiment with new flavours, new foods and drinks; finding the best independent brewer in India through a contact; people might say this was luck. But, as Bilimoria points out, without the beer idea in the first place there would have been no business. You must constantly put yourself in the position where luck presents itself, if you don't then you are not going to 'get lucky'.

On the day that Bilimoria was admitted to the House of Lords he thanked a colleague for starting him out on his journey in public life with his first public appointment in 1999. His colleague replied that it was what he made of the journey that counted.

Discipline

People often have preconceived ideas about entrepreneurs as uncontrollable, maverick, disorganised people. But in many ways, says Bilimoria, the complete opposite is true.

'Being an entrepreneur means being a self-starter – which means always taking the initiative – no one is telling you what to do,' he says. 'It is not like working in a large structured organisation where there are people telling you what do, as well as people you can consult about the proper way to carry out a task. As an entrepreneur, certainly at the start, you will be on your own for a lot of the time. And being a self-starter requires discipline.'

Hard work

Creating a successful business means always being willing to work that much harder. To keep pushing yourself. There is no substitute for hard work, drive, determination, persistence, and perseverance. If one bank manager after another says 'no', to your request for funding, keep going until you find one that says 'yes'.

Bilimoria cites the indomitable spirit of Winston Churchill encapsulated in this excerpt from one of his famous speeches: 'Never give in ... – in nothing, great or small, large or petty – never give in, except to convictions of honour and good sense.'

Hand in hand with the work ethic goes another Bilimoria requirement – high energy levels.

Foresight

By foresight Bilimoria means always looking ahead and taking a very long-term view. Whether it is using formal techniques like scenario planning, or informal methods as Cobra does with the Grand Canyon plan (see Chapter Ten).

A constant desire to learn

Continuous learning is something Bilimoria is also particularly keen on. He has taken a course at Cranfield University, annually attends courses at Harvard Business School and the London Business School, and also enables his employees to add to their knowledge and skills in the same way (see Chapter Eight).

> **BILIMORIA'S BUSINESS TIPS: STRENGTHS AND WEAKNESSES**
>
> *Know your own personal skills and weaknesses, says Bilimoria. Often a lot of entrepreneurs are not particularly good managers. There is nothing wrong with that, but if that is the case, recognise it and make sure you recruit the best managers.*

A TALENT FOR SELLING

Most start-ups begin life with very little money. Possibly some seed funding, maybe some government backed loans, whatever cash the founder, or founders, can muster. Almost certainly there will be no money for big ad agencies or marketing campaigns. So it helps to have someone on board who is good at selling.

Bilimoria is a natural salesman, although it took him some time to realise it. His sales skills weren't spotted early on, and there was little said during his schooldays to encourage him to become an entrepreneur.

It was at university that he discovered his talent for selling a product. At Cambridge University, Bilimoria stood for president of the Cambridge Union. It was a prestigious position. The snag was getting the electorate – several thousand students probably more interested in studying and having a good time than student politics – to vote for him. Ever optimistic, Bilimoria got out on the stump, tramping up and down the stairways of the various colleges, knocking on the electors' doors, pressing the flesh and soliciting support. After a vigorous campaign, he lost by just six votes. But although he lost, he realised he had a talent for persuasion. Couple that with hard work and it was almost possible to achieve the impossible. Bilimoria was eventually elected to the post of vice-president.

The benefits of salesmanship combined with a self-starter attitude were also useful when, short of cash, he offered to help out a friend with his fledgling magazine. Bilimoria was staying with his friend Richard Armstrong, who had launched a newsletter called *European Accounting Focus*. The annual subscription was £350. Armstrong was coping well with the journalistic side of things, but Bilimoria was not convinced that enough resources were being committed to the sale and marketing of subscriptions. After persuading his friend and landlord that he was the man to handle this side of things, Bilimoria parked himself at the kitchen table every morning and got on the phone. He proved an extremely effective salesman and in one month alone sold 70 subscriptions.

USEFUL EXPERIENCE

Many entrepreneurs may dismiss the idea of doing an MBA. Surely any budding business founder should be out there getting on with it? Yet there are many entrepreneurs who believe in the benefits of business related education to complement the practical hands-on business experience, whether it is an MBA, other masters qualification, or accountancy exams. As we know, Bilimoria believes in continual learning and, as he readily admits, his education was wonderful preparation for his future career.

Before Bilimoria committed to life as an entrepreneur, he trained as an accountant. First he studied in India, then in England. When he travelled to England after completing a conversion course he joined accountancy firm Arthur Young (later Ernst & Young), situated just off Fleet Street. The London office alone employed 2000 people and while Bilimoria did not enjoy working for such a large organisation, he came to value the experience that it gave him.

'A lot of entrepreneurs have never worked in a large organisation, so working at the accountancy firm allowed me to experience working in a professional environment,' he says. 'It helped instil discipline. At the end of the week, for example, we filled out a timesheet on which we had to account for every 15 minutes of our time.'

Bilimoria also went on a number of internal training courses, including one on instructional techniques, which led to him becoming an instructor on various courses, something he enjoyed doing. By the end of his first year he was obviously well thought of by his superiors, because they took the unusual step of entrusting someone so relatively inexperienced with instructing on the month-long induction course for new graduates.

Apart from learning his craft, Bilimoria was also learning about business in general through his regular visits to client companies for audits. These ranged in size and competence from small companies who presented him with a box full of papers that forced him to prepare the accounts from scratch to rather more sophisticated multinationals. In this way he became familiar with the workings of companies such as Suzuki, and the Heron petrol station chain and property group.

It was his involvement with his largest private client, an aeronautical company called Marshalls, which not only owned Cambridge Airport but designed the revolutionary nose of the Concorde and had a number of contracts from the Ministry of Defence, that made the biggest impression on him. It was run by a man with all the instincts of the successful entrepreneur and Bilimoria was entranced. 'It was fascinating, absolutely fascinating,' he recalls. 'That aspect of my chartered accountancy training was perfect. The other thing with chartered accountancy is that it's a people business. It is actually about dealing with people. Leading a team – an audit team – and working within clients' companies involves getting information from people, quite often dealing with sensitive issues.'

As an entrepreneur, it is important to know you own mind, stick to your plan and resist the allure of a more structured career path – and salary progression. As the months passed, Bilimoria began to understand how easy it was for people to get sucked into climbing the career ladder, even those with entrepreneurial spirit. Yet while a partnership in an accountancy practice was tempting, Bilimoria felt that he didn't quite fit.

He recalls an interesting exchange towards the end of his qualifying period: 'I remember once at that end of an audit, we were all sitting around in the office and our boss at the time said he was going to tell each one of us what he thought we were really good at, and what we should be doing in the future. He said at least 50 per cent of us would leave because they have to accept that certain people will leave straight after qualifying. When it came to me, he said I would be very good at marketing.' It was an extremely prescient remark.

The exposure to Cambridge through his work on the Marshalls account also made Bilimoria decide Cambridge University was where he wanted to complete the next stage of his education after qualifying as a chartered accountant, rather than Harvard Business School, where he had considered applying to do an MBA. 'I fell in love with Cambridge on that audit,' says Bilimoria. 'I went there twice a year, every year.' The qualifications he had already obtained meant that he could complete his law degree in two years rather than three. Determined to go to Cambridge, he managed to secure a place to do Law, and, with the help of a loan, headed up to Cambridge and Sidney Sussex College.

THE SPIRIT OF THE ENTREPRENEUR

Having successfully completed his degree, Bilimoria returned to London.

KARAN'S BUSINESS TIPS:
NEGOTIATING?

Negotiating, says Bilimoria, is invariably a compromise, but the compromise should end up being one where people walk away feeling reasonably happy. 'If you feel too happy, then maybe the other person is miserable, which is not a good thing,' he says. 'I think there is that element of fairness, and if it is a fair deal, a fair transaction, both people should feel reasonably happy. It is that whole element of always leaving something on the table for the other person.'

He applied for a number of jobs in the City and eventually found one as a consulting accountant with financial services company Cresvale. His heart wasn't in it, however: his entrepreneurial instincts ran too deep. Within months, he had resigned and embarked on a new career as an entrepreneur.

Given the harsh realities of life that confronted Bilimoria following his graduation in the summer of 1988, this ambition soon began to look like nothing more than a romantic daydream. Not only did he not have any money, but he had accumulated £20,000 of student debt and had no visible means of support. Determined to make it as an entrepreneur, he had given up his job. That said, he was realistic enough to accept that commencing operations with a national beer brand was overambitious: 'I thought, "Hang on, this is going to be a huge project. I'm going to require a lot of capital to do this and I have no money." I realised that the beer project would have to wait while I built up some experience and capital.'

Entrepreneurs may need certain attributes to succeed; they may be able to acquire some skills and knowledge through education, at a business school or elsewhere. There is, however, no substitute for business experience. Many famous entrepreneurs tried out a number of different business ideas before arriving at the one that they are most closely associated with. Richard Branson ran a student newspaper before launching Virgin Records. The legendary advertising executive David Ogilvy worked as an AGA cooker salesman, as a pollster for Dr. George Gallup, and as a tobacco farmer with an Amish community in Pennsylvania, before starting his own advertising agency. Bilimoria was no exception.

'I had no money and no business experience,' says Bilimoria. 'The lager beer had to wait, I needed to build up some experience, so I started some new projects.'

Bilimoria's first foray into business was importing polo sticks. Traditionally, polo players in Britain used sticks sourced from Argentina. The Falklands war between the UK and Argentina put paid to that, however. With a trade embargo still in force there was a shortage of polo sticks and a market opportunity to exploit.

The obvious solution was to import sticks from India. Bilimoria learned to play polo back in India; he was good enough to earn a half-blue playing for Cambridge University, and lead the University side on a tour of India. From his experience playing polo, he considered the Indian product superior. Made with bamboo heads rather than the conventional willow, Indian polo sticks were whippier and springier than the Argentinian version. They were also extremely cheap. Bilimoria could buy them for £1 and sell them to a retailer like Harrods, for example, for £15.

Initial enthusiasm was dampened after a disappointing meeting with an assistant buyer at the Knightsbridge store. Not for the first time, however, Bilimoria refused to be discouraged. Together with Arjun Reddy, an old family friend, (see box opposite) he formed A & K International Ltd (AKI, after the initials of their first names), in February 1989. A subsequent meeting with the assistant buyer's boss proved more successful, Harrods placed an order, and the pair eventually sold close to 300 polo sticks to the store.

Despite the Harrod's polo sticks account, money remained in short supply and Bilimoria and Reddy were forced to look at other possibilities. Over a period of several months they expanded their business to include, among other items, pearls from Hyderabad, towels from Bombay, and luxury leather goods. They also imported silk jackets hand-embroidered with gold and sequins which were sold in high-end boutiques in the UK.

For the moment the beer business would have to wait.

COBRA COMMENT:
ARJUN REDDY – FORMER BUSINESS PARTNER

When we first started importing Cobra, there were just the two of us! We were equal partners in the business, so we both did everything, from working with the brewery in India, to opening accounts with Indian restaurants and meeting distributors. We would often go down to the P&O bonded warehouse in Canning Town in the East End to collect the beer for delivery.

In the early days we also did quite a few deliveries ourselves in an old 2CV Citroen which Karan nicknamed Albert. I hated the wretched car and Karan would become quite upset if I said anything about it. I must say it never let us down; though, with its unique suspension, with a full load of beer it did have a funny habit of lurching and hopping down the road like a kangaroo. We would pile the car full of beer and I think without a co-pilot we could get up to 16 cases.

I still feel quite proud of the fact that I can say I sold the first case of Cobra, it was to The Chelsea Tandoori – I think it was five cases.

What makes Cobra special as a business?
We capitalised on the niche market of selling to the Indian restaurants, this was our initial base to start with. Many other beer brands were launched and failed when we first started. We were fortunate to have that solid base.

What aspect of the Cobra business would you hold up as best practice to other entrepreneurs and business owners?
The ability and resolve to hang in there and believe in your product and yourself. Cobra has taken close to 20 years to be where it is today and that's a long journey of many highs and lows.

Could you recall one memory or story of your experiences with Cobra that defines the Karan Bilimoria and Cobra approach to business?
At the time we started Cobra, Karan and I lived together on Fulham Palace Road. One morning we awoke to realise we had just about run out of money. We decided to sum up the hopelessness of the situation and literally emptied our pockets on the dining room table. Together we had less than four pounds.

Fortunately, we had a meeting scheduled with our bank manager at Lloyds bank on Edgware road that same day. We set off for that meeting armed with some notes and a rough cash flow calculation. On a jam packed tube somewhere near Fulham Broadway, Karan, who was reading the cash flow, decided the numbers were not right. He felt there was more room for inflating the forecasted sales figures. Since it was a crowded train, he had nowhere to sit down and make the changes so he put the sheet against my back and rewrote the figures.

We got the loan increase; I believe it was £9000 pounds.

Karan always had the determination to push through even when there was no light in sight. This ability alone, more than anything else I believe made Cobra the success it is.

CHAPTER TWO

FIRST STEPS

S tarting out as an entrepreneur can be a trying time, eking out a meagre existence, plagued by self-doubt. It is at moments like these that confidence in your own abilities and your original vision becomes crucial.

STICK WITH IT

A limited trade in polo sticks, towels and other items kept Bilimoria afloat financially. But only just. His parents watched his progress with some disapproval, especially given the fact that had a professional accountancy qualification, plus a degree in law from one of the most prestigious universities in the world. Yet despite his prestigious education he was struggling to make ends meet and working in import/export.

It was then that one of those 'lucky' moments occurred. Bilimoria and Reddy had hatched a plan to import seafood. The first part of the plan involved getting hold of some product brochures through a family friend. But when the brochure arrived, Bilimoria was less interested in the shellfish than he was in the corporate tagline on the last page: 'Pals Seafood is a division of Mysore breweries. Brewers of the famous Pals Beer.'

Bilimoria quickly forgot about seafood and focused on the beer. He contacted the owner of Pals and asked if he would be interested in exporting Pals to the UK. To his surprise the owner said yes.

The Mysore Brewery was a formidable partner to have. A former Coca-Cola bottling plant, it had grown to become the biggest privately owned brewer in India. It was run by Mr K. P. Balasubramanium (known as Mr Balan), the son of the founder, a man called Palani – hence Pals. The family started with the Pals brand, but the business really took off when they launched a premium brand called Knockout. It was eight per cent alcohol by volume (ABV) – its label showed one boxer standing over another he had knocked to the canvas. As strong beer became more and more popular, sales of Knockout soon outstripped the weaker Pals beer, which was four per cent ABV. To this day, 70 per cent of beer sold in India is strong beer.

Mr Balan may have said 'yes', to Bilimoria's request, which was a start, but Bilimoria still faced a significant challenge to get the beer imported into the UK.

The problems began with Bilimoria's attempts get samples of the beer delivered to him in London. After battling through a forest of red tape, a consignment was air-freighted via British Airways. But, by the time the beer landed in the UK, all the bottles were broken. In the end, he had to persuade a friend to bring over a few bottles in his hand luggage.

When the bottles arrived Bilimoria discovered problem number two: neither of the Mysore beers had the taste that he was looking for. He wanted a premium lager that combined the smoothness of real ale with the refreshing qualities of a lager; one that was about five per cent ABV. Not the four per cent Pals, or the eight per cent Knockout. Then there was the issue of the brand names. Pals was too similar to the popular brand of pet food, Pal. As for Knockout, there was no chance the UK Trading Standards would allow that name to be used for a beer brand.

It was a daunting prospect, but it was obvious that the only way forward was for Bilimoria and Reddy to come up with a brand of their own, and for the Mysore Brewery to produce an entirely new recipe to their specifications. So began a long and frustrating courtship by telex – the Mysore Brewery was not in possession of a fax machine in those days, and commercial email was a glint in Bill Gates' eye. An enthusiastic Bilimoria and Reddy telexed proposal after proposal through to the brewery, only to find their frustration growing with each day that passed, as they read through the telexed responses, and the one phrase that appeared with increasing regularity: 'Not possible in India ...'

HOW A DANISH LAGER CAME TO DOMINATE INDIAN RESTAURANTS

When Karan Bilimoria was mulling over the possibility of producing his curry-friendly beer in the late Eighties, the brand that dominated the Indian restaurant scene was Carlsberg.

The story of how a Danish lager became the drink of choice to accompany Indian food centres on one King of Denmark's fondness for the Veeraswamy, London's oldest Indian, founded in 1927 at the premises it still occupies on Swallow Street, off Regent Street.

Legend has it that the monarch from Copenhagen so loved the restaurant, its food and the hospitality he received there that he made a point of sending a present of a case of Carlsberg to the Veeraswamy every year. And so, when Carlsberg became widely available in the UK, the Veeraswamy began stocking it and, as it was the model for so many Indian restaurants that followed, they stocked it too.

'You'd get a waiter and a chef breaking away and opening up their own restaurant because they could see that Veeraswamy was successful,' observes Bilimoria. 'They took the view that they must do exactly what the Veeraswamy had been doing, including the menu and of course the drinks. They would say, "We have to have Carlsberg".'

At the time of the launch of Kingfisher in the early Eighties and Cobra in 1990, Carlsberg was still a 'must stock' item among Indian restaurants. And, in those days, 90 per cent of Carlsberg sold was in the form of draught Carlsberg Pils or Carlsberg Export.

PASSAGE TO INDIA

Sometimes it is just not possible to work things out remotely. Even today in a world of email, Skype, videoconferencing and mobile phones, many senior executives prefer face-to-face meetings. For Bilimoria, email or video conferencing was not an option. The only way to resolve the various sticking points was for Bilimoria to get on a plane and head for India.

He had just turned 28 when he took the trip to India for one of the most pivotal meetings of his business career. His meeting was with Mr Balan, owner and managing director of the Mysore Brewery in Bangalore. It was the best opportunity that he would have to secure a brewery contract.

The Mysore brewery was doing extremely well at the time. Bilimoria presented himself at reception, and was led through the opulent headquarters building and up several floors, to where Mr Balan was waiting to greet him.

With the introductions over, Balan led Bilimoria into the office where the meeting was taking place. He was expecting one or two executives possibly, and a positive reception, especially as the brewer had seemed very keen about his proposals.

There, in a room roughly the size of a tennis court, the entire management team of the brewery sat in a semi-circle waiting for Bilimoria: the vice president; the company secretary; the chief accountant; the chief engineer; the head brewer – Dr Cariapa; and the general manager.

After showing Bilimoria to the hot seat facing his team, Mr Balan walked behind his desk and sat down. It was Bilimoria's first real taste of corporate deal making and negotiations.

'I felt very much on my own,' recalls Bilimoria. 'I had never met these people before, ever in my life. I was 28 years old, with no money, and no experience. And they knew that. To sum it up, they all, individually and collectively, laughed in my face.

'Their whole attitude was, "Look. Who are you? What makes you think you are going to succeed? All our competitors have tried to export to England and have failed – except one, Kingfisher – and even they stopped exporting. They are now brewing it over there. We know lots of other breweries are doing it and we have heard they are not doing very well. We are doing extremely well over here and you have no money, no experience of this industry, you don't know anything about manufacturing, you have never sold a bottle of beer in your life. What makes you think you are going to succeed?" '

The atmosphere in the room had been oppressive from the start. Everyone was in shirt-sleeves as the ceiling fans fought a losing battle to offer some relief from the humid south Indian summer. No one was feeling the heat more than Bilimoria, as he listened to his brilliant business idea and his abilities being pulled to pieces.

It was all completely unexpected. Bilimoria had spent months lobbying the brewery via telephone and telex. He had gone to great lengths to emphasise how popular imported lagers had become in the UK. Sol beer from Mexico was showing signs of becoming a major brand, Singha was being imported from Thailand, Budvar and Pilsner Urquell from the Czech Republic, and Budweiser from the United States. The British were waking up to the fact that lager need not be synonymous with 'fizzy' and 'bland', but could have flavour, character and history. No one in the room, other than himself, seemed to remember any of this.

Recovering himself with an effort, Bilimoria embarked on a spirited defence of his project. Even today he remembers exactly what he said to them. 'I said, "I know I am going to succeed, because I have faith in what I am going to be doing, and I have confidence in myself because I have come up with an idea of producing a beer that is going to be different, that is going to be better, and that is going to change the marketplace I am going into forever," he recalls. "I have faith that this product of mine, because of its qualities, is going to perform very well. I am certain I have found a niche in the market that nobody else is fulfilling."'

Bilimoria continued by outlining his idea to produce a beer to accompany Indian food, a beer that would appeal to ale drinkers and lager drinkers alike. He told them that he wanted to brew it in India and then export it to Britain so it would have the appropriate air of authenticity.

Convincing though his pitch was, made with such evident self-belief, passion and confidence, he still only swayed two of his interrogators, who began to doubt their earlier scepticism and instead believe that the young entrepreneur in front of them just might be onto something. Fortunately for Bilimoria, the two individuals concerned were probably the two most important people there with respect to his proposal. One was Balan, the owner of the brewery; the other was Cariapa, the chief brewer.

As owner, Balan's support was crucial; however, in many ways Cariapa's was even more important. The youngest person to earn a PhD in brewing from Prague University, Cariapa had gone on to spend six years in the Czech Republic working for the world-famous Pilsner Urquell. At the time of his collaboration with Bilimoria, he was in his late 30s, and a dynamic man with a passion for beer-making. It is an interesting example of how it is not always the most obvious people who are the most critical to the success of an enterprise. Bilimoria describes Cariapa as a 'key, key person' in the Cobra story. If Bilimoria is the father of Cobra beer, then Cariapa is the obstetrician.

KARAN'S BUSINESS TIPS:
NEVER TAKE 'NO' FOR AN ANSWER

'When you are starting in business, the word you come across more than anything else is the word "No". And what you have to do is turn that word "No" into a "Yes", whether you are selling door-to-door, or trying to develop something, the initial reaction you are going to get from people is, "No".

'You have to come to expect it because when you know it is coming you can prepare strategies to deal with it. Why is it that Lance Armstrong has won the Tour de France seven times, something no one else had done?

'I believe it is his mental attitude, and I believe from what I have heard, that the only way to win the Tour de France is on the uphills. And I am convinced that when all the other riders see the uphills, they say, "Oh dear, here come the uphills", and I am convinced that Lance Armstrong says, "Here come the uphills, this is my opportunity to win. I know they are coming, I know they're coming, this is my opportunity to win".

'It is the same with that word "No". You know it is coming, so don't get disheartened. Your job is to convert that "No" into a "Yes". Your job is to convert threats to opportunities. Your job is to convert frustration to opportunity. Your job is to convert obstacles into opportunities. And you learn to do that throughout building a business.'

EXPECT THE UNEXPECTED

Having secured the co-operation of the Mysore Brewery, Bilimoria settled down for an extended stay in Bangalore. For three months, Bilimoria and Cariapa tested various combinations of barley malt, yeast, rice, maize and hops, until, by a process of trial and error, they came up with a taste that Bilimoria was happy with.

Now the beer was ready to go into production. Bilimoria's next step was to source the bottles. The average Indian beer bottle is a relatively fragile entity due to the recycling process that keeps the market going. To make its

long journey from the brewery in Bangalore to the
Indian restaurants in the UK, and remain intact, the
beer would need to be stored in much more robust
bottles.

Through his network of family contacts Bilimoria
got in touch with the managing director of the biggest bottle manufacturer in India, based in Hyderabad. The company agreed to produce special bottles
for Bilimoria, but there was another snag – the size
of the bottles. At the time, most beer in the UK was
sold in 330ml bottles, but the standard size in India
was 650ml – a much bigger bottle, and one that the
brewery insisted on using as they were not bottling 330ml at all at that time.
Reluctantly Bilimoria went ahead and placed his order.

> **KARAN'S BUSINESS TIPS:
> BUILDING THE BRAND**
> *'Our most valuable asset is
> the Cobra beer brand,' says
> Bilimoria. 'Always, always
> start your own brand if you
> can, or you end up being
> an agent or distributor.
> And with a brand you can
> build value.'*

It would be nice to think that that was the last of the obstacles between
Bilimoria and the initial launch of Cobra beer. Certainly there would be
many ups and down to come as the company grew. Most are related in this
book. But with the idea well thought out, the brewery signed up, the product
developed, the bottles agreed, what more could get in the way?

Bilimoria soon found out. As far as Bilimoria had travelled en route to getting a new Indian brewed beer onto the tables of Indian restaurants in the
UK, there was some way still to go, and many more obstacles.

Take the Excise Authority, for example. In India each state was entitled to
charge duty on alcohol being produced or consumed in the state. As a result
a law was passed that forced all beer bottle labels to display the name of the
state in which they could be sold – if the beer was being exported from Karnataka to Maharashtra (another state in India), for instance, the label would
have to declare 'not for sale in Karnataka. For sale in Maharashtra only', Bilimoria's beer was being brewed in India but could not be sold in any of the
states, as it was intended for export. Consequently the law required it to list
both that it was not for sale in Karnataka, where Bangalore is situated, and
also that it was for export only. Bilimoria did not want to state that the beer
was not for sale in Karnataka. It would only confuse the customer in England
and take up valuable space on the label, especially given that the beer had
only one label – no back or neck label.

It took a visit to the Excise Commissioner, unannounced, to find an acceptable solution. 'I just walked into his office – one of the most important men in the state – and told him the facts,' says Bilimoria. 'I wasn't going to let the License Raj defeat me.' In the end they agreed a compromise wording.

And what about distribution back in England? It was one thing to arrange production, but the product still needed distributing. So Bilimoria and Reddy hastily negotiated an agreement with Lyne Zilkha, the woman responsible for distributing the Czech Budweiser in the UK, to handle the beer in the south of England, and with Jeff Hind of Brent Walker to look after it in the north. Sitting down with Lotus Notes 1-2-3, Bilimoria did some quick spreadsheet calculations and predicted that he would send the distributors two containers of 1375 cases each every month. This figure would rise to ten containers a month within five years, he forecast.

KARAN'S BUSINESS TIPS:
NEGOTIATE TIGHT CONTRACTS

Bilimoria may believe in trust and doing business on a handshake. But when the contracts are drawn up he believes in eliminating the wriggle room. In an ideal world contracts would be drawn up, signed, put on file and never consulted again until the time comes to renew them, he says. But it is always best to consider the worst-case scenario when the agreement is being negotiated.

'The contract should always be very tightly drawn, however good your relationship with the other party, because the person you are sitting across the table from may leave for whatever reason,' he says. 'They may retire, they may be fired, they may move on, and you will be left to deal with somebody else with whom you may not have the same relationship. That's when you are reliant on that contract. And so it is very, very important to always have a strong, good, tight contract, particularly when you are dealing with very large organisations where people are constantly being moved on or promoted or simply leave.'

A LESS GASSY BEER BY ANY OTHER NAME (THAN PANTHER)

Everything was set. The beer was about two weeks away from bottling. The distributors were signed up. It was a lovely evening. Bilimoria was happy. And then the phone rang. It was Reddy, his partner, and he was in a panic.

The distributors had been pre-selling the beer and there was a problem. No one liked the name. Bilimoria had written a list of hundreds of possible names, they had spent countless hours whittling the list down until just one remained – Panther. Informal tasting showed that people loved the beer. They just hated the name.

Bilimoria was completely thrown. The artwork was with the printing press. The labels were due to be printed – thousands of them. 'We had two options,' says Bilimoria. 'Either we decided to stick with the name we had chosen, regardless of what people thought, and make the name work. The alternative was to try another name.'

Bilimoria said he would contact the printers in the morning on the off chance that they hadn't printed the labels yet. In the meantime, asked Bilimoria, what was number two on the list of names? Cobra, replied Reddy. So Bilimoria told him to try Cobra with the consumers and the distributors, and get back to Bilimoria as soon as he could, but by no later than two days.

Fortunately, far from having the printed all the labels already, the print shop had yet to print any of them. Stop the press, said Bilimoria. Next, Reddy rang with some good news. Everyone liked the name Cobra.

So Bilimoria got on the phone to his brother, Nadir, who was based in Hyderabad and had founded an advertising agency start-up. He had put a small team together and the agency was just beginning to make a reputation for itself. Bilimoria explained the problem to his brother who told him to get on the next plane to Hyderabad. Two weeks before the

> **KARAN'S BUSINESS TIPS: DO YOUR CONSUMER TESTING**
>
> *The change of the beer name from Panther to Cobra caused Bilimoria a few headaches and, in the event, delayed the whole project by two weeks, but Bilimoria doesn't regret making the decision. 'The lesson I learned was, as an entrepreneur, you come up with the ideas, but never ever go forward with the ideas until you have checked them with the consumer first.'*

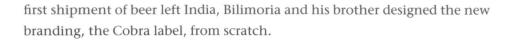

first shipment of beer left India, Bilimoria and his brother designed the new branding, the Cobra label, from scratch.

THE COBRA CAST

DYNSHAW ITALIA, ACA, FINANCE DIRECTOR AND CHIEF OPERATING OFFICER

Italia joined Cobra Beer from ebookers plc in November 2001 as finance director and took on the newly created role of chief operating officer in April 2004. He is responsible for the finance, operations, IT & HR functions of the company. At ebookers, as group financial controller then director of financial operations, Italia was heavily involved in establishing operations in 11 European countries and the group's flotation on the London Stock Exchange and NASDAQ. Prior to ebookers, Italia was at KPMG for three years.

CHRISTOPHER EDGCUMBE-RENDLE, BUSINESS DEVELOPMENT DIRECTOR

Edgcumbe-Rendle joined Cobra in February 1996 as the national accounts manager, then became the sales director. Since June 2003, he has been the new business development director with responsibility for the group's international subsidiaries, breweries, mainstream sales and new product development. Prior to joining Cobra, he owned and operated a tea and coffee trading and wholesaling company. Brought up in India as a child, he speaks fluent Hindi.

SAMSON SOHAIL (BA, B.ED), SALES DIRECTOR

Sohail joined Cobra in 1993 and was one of Cobra's first sales executives. He now heads a team selling to Indian restaurants, which includes a field sales team, a telesales team and a sales support team.

SIMON EDWARDS (MA KINGSTON), MARKETING DIRECTOR

Edwards joined Cobra in June 1998 and has been instrumental in both improving Cobra's market share in Indian restaurants, and the move into the mainstream. Prior to joining Cobra Beer, Edwards was marketing manager at EasyJeans UK Ltd – during a period in which it saw significant market share growth – and a regional marketing and sales operations manager at Courage. While working full time for Cobra, Edwards obtained a Masters in Marketing from Kingston University in 2003, graduating with Honours.

PATRICK PAINES (MA CAMBRIDGE), NON-EXECUTIVE DIRECTOR

Paines has served as a non-executive director since 1995. He is currently a consultant to UBS Private Bank; a partner at Lakeshore Capital LLP (Investment Banking), and a partner at Javelin Capital LLP, (Venture Capital). Paines has substantial City experience including as a director of NatWest Markets and SG Securities, and in corporate finance at Cazenove between 1989 and 1997. Paines currently acts as a consultant to 3C.

JAMIE BERGER (PhD HARVARD, MA CAMBRIDGE), NON-EXECUTIVE DIRECTOR

Berger has served as a non-executive director since 1995. He has a PhD from Harvard University in History and East Asian Languages.

SUNIL SHETH (LLB HONOURS), NON-EXECUTIVE DIRECTOR

Sheth has served as a non-executive director since September 2003. He is a partner with Fladgate Fielder Solicitors, and was previously a senior consultant with Merricks LLP Solicitors, and an equity partner at Bayer-Rosin Solicitors. He is also a past president of the Society of Asian Lawyers.

ANDREW LAND (LLB HONOURS, MBA), NON-EXECUTIVE DIRECTOR

Land has served as a non-executive director since July 2006. He is a principal of Och-Ziff Capital Management Group, focused on private investments. He was previously a principal of DLJ Merchant Banking Partners, the leveraged corporate buy-out group of Credit Suisse. Land is also a director of Peacocks Group Limited and Whitehead Mann Group.

SIGNIFICANT OTHERS

ROBERT KNOX (MA CAMBRIDGE, MSc BIRMINGHAM), TECHNICAL DIRECTOR

Knox joined Cobra as the group's first technical director in 2003. He was previously production director at Charles Wells. He has many years of brewing experience and has brewed in 20 countries throughout the world.

JAIMIN CHANDARANA (ACCA, AAT, CIMA), FINANCIAL CONTROLLER

Chandarana has been with Cobra since 1996, and has always played a finance role within the company. Prior to joining Cobra he was the financial controller at AT Fouks Lynch, a publishing company. He graduated from the London School of Accountancy.

PERSES BILIMORIA, REGIONAL DIRECTOR, INDIA, B.COM (HONS)

Bilimoria joined Cobra in March 2002 to launch Cobra Beer in India with the ambition to make it a mainstream beer brand in the Indian market. Bilimoria has extensive business experience, and previously was involved with a British group called Guinness Mahon plc for their trading outfit, doing exports from the UK to India. He later started an import business for specialised tires for the mining/power/cement industry. He is currently pioneering the bio-polymer industry in India.

BRUCE WALKER (HDHM), REGIONAL DIRECTOR, SOUTH AFRICA

A South African, Walker joined Cobra in 2003 as head of the company's South African subsidiary. Previously he was in the hotel industry and food and beverage distribution.

HOSHANG CHENOY (MA), VICE PRESIDENT, MARKETING, UNITED STATES

Chenoy joined Cobra in 1998, working first in the sales department and later in the chief executive's team. Moving next to the role of marketing manager, in 2003 Chenoy assumed to role of US vice president, marketing, as Cobra expanded into the American market.

CHAPTER THREE

FINANCING COBRA

O ne of the biggest challenges entrepreneurs face, unless they are fortunate enough to have very wealthy parents, is raising the finance to fund their ambitious plans to build a business empire. Most entrepreneurs start with nothing, or next to nothing. Bilimoria started with less than nothing – £20,000 of student debt.

It is not any easier to raise finance if you happen to start a business at the beginning of one of the worst recessions since World War II, which is when Cobra Beer finally got underway. The banks had clamped down on lending, and base interest rates in the UK were about 14 per cent. That Bilimoria managed to get his business out of the starting blocks, let alone create the successful business he runs today, is a considerable achievement.

As Bilimoria likes to point out, raising money is not the only challenge. The real challenge for entrepreneurs is to raise the money in a way in which they can protect and hold on to ownership of their business, especially once they have a proven concept. It is like waiting for a racehorse to run clear of the field before putting your bet on: everyone wants to back a winner.

'If you have confidence in your business, sales are growing, your brand value is growing, the value of your business is growing – then you must hold on to your shares,' says Bilimoria. 'This makes it extremely difficult to raise finance, because most investors want equity.'

Bilimoria's answer has been to turn to innovative financing methods (shown in detail on p.37). And while his accountancy background was undoubtedly useful, the list of financing methods that Cobra has benefited from is a testimony to what some imagination and determination can achieve. 'You must be innovative and persistent in raising finance from a variety of different sources and that means keeping an open mind,' he says.

KARAN'S BUSINESS TIPS:
THE CREDIBILITY GAP

A common challenge that early stage entrepreneurs face, says Bilimoria, is something he calls 'the credibility gap'. It is the situation when nobody knows you, nobody knows your brand, and nobody knows your product. In that situation what makes people supply you, finance you and buy from you?

Bilimoria believes that people will do these things if the entrepreneur has complete and utter passion, faith, belief and confidence in what they are doing – in the idea, the product, the brand – this gives people the faith to trust the entrepreneur, and give them a chance. It also helps if they can find a way to appear credible in the eyes of the person they are dealing with; this may mean different things in different situations.

Raising finance is a good example of this. When Bilimoria was raising finance for his business early on, there was a definite credibility gap. However, Bilimoria managed to narrow that gap. First, he was a chartered accountant which gave the bankers a certain level of comfort concerning his financial aptitude. His first bank overdraft was completely unsecured.

Second, going forward, he hired good advisors. 'When you are a small business, the temptation is to try to keep your costs really low,' says Bilimoria. 'But this often means that entrepreneurs are scared to go for the best advisors, because they are worried that they are going to be too expensive. Of course the excellent advice that you get is expensive, but the credibility you get from working with a top advisor makes it worth the expense.'

Bilimoria hired Grant Thornton as accountants and found that the credibility Cobra got from the association with one of the UK's top firms of accountants opened doors to investors and banks. So it is a false economy not to get the best advice.

A LARGE OVERDRAFT

In the early months at Cobra it was possible for Bilimoria to run the company first using an overdraft facility, and then using a £55,000 loan through a government backed loan scheme. It was obvious, however, that with the beer supply secured and the containers steadily making their way to the UK, £55,000 was not going to last for long.

By the beginning of 1991 the beer was reaching 100 restaurants – 1000 cases of 650ml per month – way outstripping Bilimoria's Lotus projections. After some initial problems securing a distributor, Bilimoria and Reddy approached Gandhi Oriental Foods in Bow, East London, to act as a distributor for Cobra. The firm agreed, eventually. It was even prepared to receive containers of beer direct from Southampton port and offload the cases onto pallets. Potentially this was a company-making deal for Cobra. There was just one hitch. Gandhi was in a position of power and, with a superb credit rating, expected 60 days credit. It had no intention of paying cash on delivery.

Cobra, on the other hand, had no credit rating as such. Nor did it have sufficient funds to pay for a container load of beer, deliver it to Gandhi and then wait two months to get the money back. Bilimoria was faced with a dilemma. Gandhi was the key to moving the business to the next level, it had finally agreed to be a distributor, yet Cobra couldn't fund the ongoing business on the credit terms proposed. Gandhi also wanted the exclusive distribution rights for Indian restaurants in Greater London.

Bilimoria was not that easily discouraged though. Drawing on his experience as an accountant he came up with an ingenious solution. Gandhi was a very well run family company – maybe it had unused overdraft facilities. His instincts were right: Gandhi was completely debt-free, with an unutilised overdraft of £1m.

'I told them I had a way where Gandhi could have its 60 days credit and I could still get my cash on delivery,' he says. 'And I used an old text book instrument called a bill of exchange. It is one of the first things you learn about when you study accounting.'

Bilimoria's plan was as follows. Once a container-load of Cobra had been delivered and unloaded, the Gandhi would sign a bill of exchange: 'I promise to pay in 60 days' whatever the relevant sum was. Arjun and Karan would then take the bill of exchange to Gandhi's bank, Barclays, where a 'blocked overdraft facility' for, say, £100,000 would have been arranged. Barclays stamped the bill of exchange utilising this facility, and in effect guaranteed payment of the bill in 60 days. Arjun and Karan would then present the bill of exchange at the NatWest, where Cobra banked, and the money would appear in the Cobra account that same day.

Barclays was happy because it had a guarantee from a highly reliable customer that the money would be paid in 60 days, Gandhi was happy because Cobra was paying the fee incurred for using the previously unutilised overdraft facility and they had obtained exclusivity for the Greater London area for Cobra distributed to Indian restaurants, and Cobra was happy because it was effectively getting cash on delivery for a relatively low fee.

'In other instances, if a client is giving you credit of 45 days but you actually need 90 days, somebody can probably come in and give you that 90 days credit,' he argues. 'Obviously it costs you, but it gives you that extra credit.'

In this case, Bilimoria's inspired solution of securing the £100,000 bill of exchange discount facility paid off almost immediately. The Gandhis began to take a container-load of Cobra every month. In doing so, they doubled Cobra's sales volume. 'It was down to Gandhi's power and ability in distribution. To this day, it is one of our biggest customers in the supply chain. It got to the stage later on with Gandhi where, if we needed cash desperately in the business for whatever reason, they would pay us for the containers in advance because of the close relationship and trust between us.'

Bilimoria says, 'Whenever you are confronted with a problem in life – any time in life – always, always keep a wide perspective. You have got to be innovative. We are not talking about creative accounting here, we are talking about remaining open minded and keeping a wide perspective.' Too often, he argues, entrepreneurs allow themselves to be bullied into giving up too much equity too early, or think the only other solution is a bank loan when there are, in fact, a host of other possible options.

FUNDING GROWTH

With the business going well, Cobra began to be approached by some of the larger accountancy firms. Until the summer of 1993, Cobra's tax planning and auditing was handled by Haynes Watts – then ranked about 20 in the country – based in Slough.

Other tax issues and corporate finance were handled by a sole practitioner called Dr Sanjiv Talwar, who Bilimoria describes as 'probably the most qualified accountant in the country, if not the world'. Apart from having qualified as both a chartered accountant and a cost and management accountant, he was a gold medallist in economics from St Stephen's College in Delhi, and had a PhD from the London School of Economics. He had opened up his own practice after working in corporate finance at KPMG.

Bilimoria had begun by keeping the management accounts himself, but as the company grew, he handed over the book-keeping to first Haynes Watts and later Dr Talwar. Then he was introduced to Anuj Chande, a young Asian partner at Grant Thornton. At the time, Grant Thornton was bubbling under what in those days was the Big Eight, today the Big Four, and was growing fast. Grant Thornton would play an important part in the company's next growth phase.

It was soon clear towards the end of 1993 that the company needed to raise at least £250,000 to fund the next phase of expansion. Before this the biggest lump sum Cobra had secured was a £55,000 loan under the small firms' loan guarantee scheme. The scheme is designed by the Department of Trade and Industry (the DTI) to enable people with good ideas, but no collateral, to raise up to £250,000 in the form of a bank loan.

SMALL FIRMS LOAN GUARANTEE SCHEME

The scheme is, says Bilimoria, a great way for the government to help small business start-ups.

The finer points of the scheme, as of 2006, are as follows:

- The government guarantees the lender 75 per cent of the loan amount.
- The borrower pays a two per cent premium on the outstanding balance of the loan, payable to the DTI.
- Loans of up to £250,000 can be guaranteed and with terms of up to ten years.
- The scheme is availability to qualifying UK businesses with an annual turnover of up to £5.6million that are up to five years old. This is generally determined for a company by the date the business came within the charge of corporation tax or, for a self-employed individual, when they became liable to pay class 2 National Insurance contributions.

For more details see: www.businesslink.gov.uk

KARAN'S BUSINESS TIPS:
PAY TOP RATES FOR THE BEST ADVICE

Bilimoria went through many lean periods in the course of building his company but one area where he never scrimped was on hiring the best advisers around. Whether they were lawyers, accountants, designers or advertising agencies, he always went for the best.

As he says: 'There are always going to be times when you get a bill from some advisors and you say, "Wow, that's expensive", but always work with the best advisors regardless of the cost.

'You get what you pay for, and they give you credibility. It's well worth paying for the quality of their advice and their connections and the earlier you can do it the better. We wouldn't be where we are today without the support of Grant Thornton, for example.'

Cobra's first loan was for £55,000, so it was still entitled to raise a further £195,000 using the scheme. But there was a snag. Although the scheme allowed a business to borrow up to £250,000 there was still the challenge of finding someone to lend the money. Banks were not queuing up to lend. Although the scheme protected the lender against 85 per cent of any default (now 75 per cent), they were at risk for the balance of the loan. Plus the bank only made a small margin on the repayments. Consequently banks were often reluctant to advance the money.

The person who approved the £55,000 loan obtained from NatWest had retired so that avenue was no longer an option. Bilimoria began to wonder whether he would ever find a bank manager prepared to loan him the money.

The loan was not the only option on the table. Cobra's accountants Grant Thornton knew a venture capitalist that would put up the entire amount. The catch was that the venture capitalist would receive 33 per cent of the company in return. Bilimoria rejected this approach, preferring to exhaust the bank loan route first. This was when the benefit of having good advisors became apparent. Grant Thornton introduced him to the man running the Ealing branch of the Midland bank (now HSBC) – Andrei Warhaftig.

Warhaftig asked how much Bilimoria thought his business was worth. One million pounds, replied the Cobra boss. So Warhaftig told him that if he could prove that at least one investor agreed with his valuation of the company and raise £50,000 by selling five per cent of his equity, then the Midland would lend him the balance of £195,000.

It was the best offer that Bilimoria had received and so he set about finding someone willing to take a five per cent stake of his business for £50,000. This was where Bilimoria's network of contacts and advisors proved useful. Chande knew a potential investor, Pierre Brahm. Brahm had a very successful estate agency and a substantial property portfolio. He invested in Cobra in October 1993. Bilimoria counts Chande and Brahm as two key figures in the Cobra success story.

The loan came through in December, the day before Bilimoria's wedding day, making the happiest day of his life that much happier. Especially as he avoided giving up a third of his company.

'Look at the difference,' says Bilimoria. 'We raised the £250,000 by, in effect, giving away five per cent where the venture capitalist wanted 33 per cent. I have nothing against venture capitalists, but we have never used them because, quite often, especially in the early days, you have to be prepared to give away a huge proportion of your equity.'

KARAN'S BUSINESS TIPS:
DELEGATING

It wasn't until 2001 that Cobra appointed a finance director. Until that time the role had been fulfilled by Bilimoria. He was the chief executive, as well as the finance director. It is typical of the situation at many start-ups, where the founder takes on more than one role. Usually, however, reasonably early on the founder delegates his responsibilities by hiring specialist managers for the different functions, such as operations, marketing, IT, finance etc.

Bilimoria had appointed a chief accountant some time ago, but, with his accountancy background he still assumed responsibility for raising finance, major negotiations with banks, even meetings with the auditors.

By 2001, however, it was clear that the company was expanding so quickly that Bilimoria couldn't cope with being both chief executive and finance director. With the help of company accountants Grant Thornton and his personal network of contacts Bilimoria sourced Dynshaw Italia for the FD role.

Italia was well qualified for the job. Previously he had worked as CFO at ebookers, the internet holiday and flights booking agency. He had been with ebookers from its inception and prepared it for a listing on the London Stock Exchange and the NASDAQ.

'He was a godsend,' says Bilimoria. 'He came in and took a huge weight off me. By taking on the FD role he freed me up. It also shows the huge impact that a new member of a team can bring. He set up our new systems, financial controls, an audit committee, a remuneration committee, and corporate governance procedures. We are – for all practical purposes – run as though we were a listed company.' It is ideal preparation for a company that plans to list by the end of the decade.

The new FD has also made a difference to the lives of Cobra's employees by setting up a share option scheme. Every employee of Cobra, who has been in the company for more than one year, automatically becomes a member of the share option scheme.

In fact Bilimoria was so pleased with his new FD that he made him chief operating officer as well.

WHEN THE CASH FLOW DRIES UP

It was a major step forward for the company when Bilimoria succeeded in securing £250,000 of financing for Cobra. However, the business still needed funding on a day to day basis. For many fast growing companies maintaining adequate cash flow is a perennial issue. Companies adopt different approaches to dealing with the thorny problem of cash flow. As with so many other aspects of his business Bilimoria's solution was a little unorthodox, or at least unfashionable.

Bilimoria is a great fan of the relatively unfashionable world of debtor finance. Just as he was prepared to cover the administration fee for utilising Gandhi's overdraft facility, he was also willing to pay a middleman to advance him money on the strength of his invoices, something known as factoring or invoice discounting.

'If you've got to invest in a lot of plant or you need to invest in a lot of advertising or marketing up front, it is great working capital growth finance,' he argues. The attraction of the method is that the company gives its debtors away as security to a factoring or invoice discounting company, leaving the rest of its security with the company's usual bankers. This enables the company to develop a relationship with a completely separate bank or separate factoring or invoice discounting company, while continuing a conventional banking relationship with respect to other forms of finance, such as an overdraft or secured loans.

While it does have the attraction of getting the money in quickly, there are two significant downsides to the process. It is expensive and, in the case of factoring, your customer will be aware of what you are doing.

The expense lies in the long list of fees charged. Apart from levying a hefty three to five per cent to administer the collection of debts, factoring companies charge interest on the amount advanced before the debt is redeemed, and yet another fee for the cost of insuring the debt. In return for this, the usual arrangement sees the client getting only 75 per cent of his invoice value up front, the remaining 25 per cent falling due when the factor himself has been paid.

Another negative aspect is that, while factoring is seen as a way of financing growth in many parts of the world, in the UK it is often associated with companies in trouble. Despite this, Bilimoria considers it a very good form of finance for young, growing businesses with a good debtor book and he has fond memories of his first factors, the Bibby Shipping Line, which had a factoring division in Boreham Wood.

Invoice finance is the upmarket form of factoring because the company employing it does not declare on its invoices that it is raising finance on them, companies generally have to be turning over at least £1m a year to qualify for the service, and the quality of the debtors is expected to be better.

Because the company advancing the money against the invoices is not chasing the debts – under invoice finance this remains the duty of the borrower – it charges lower fees than a factor and a more competitive rate of interest. It is also likely to advance up to 85 per cent of the value of the invoice rather than a factoring company's 75 per cent.

'We graduated to invoice financing eventually in 1996, and use it to this day,' says Bilimoria. 'We have worked with a variety of invoice factoring and invoice financing firms and what you again find is that you tend to outgrow your advisors of different sorts. With factoring and invoice finance, there have been times when we have become too big for a factoring company that was used to advancing a quarter to half a million pounds, and then is suddenly confronted with somebody wanting a million, let alone three or four or five million.'

One thing that Bilimoria is certain of, this type of debtor financing is a highly under-utilised form of finance with enormous growth potential worldwide. 'To this day, when I give my lectures at the Cranfield School of Management, I regularly give a lecture on raising finance for growing businesses,' says Bilimoria. 'If I ask a room full of 50–60 owners/managers whether they have ever used factoring or invoice discounting, only three hands out of 50 or 60 will go up.'

INNOVATIVE FINANCING METHODS

Cobra's most recent major finance emphasises the company's innovative use of financing. In July 2006, Cobra raised £27.5m. Of that sum £25m was raised via PIK – payment in kind – notes from hedge fund Och-Ziff Capital Management. The balance of £2.5m is conventional equity through a share issue to both private and institutional investors. From the £27.5m, after costs of about £1.5m, and £13m used to redeem existing convertible preference shares, some £13m remained to invest in growing the business.

The fundraising valued the company at £80m before new money, or about £100m including debt.

RETAINING OWNERSHIP

A company growing as quickly as Cobra Beer soon gets through £250,000. The company signed a six month trial distribution deal with a large distributor – Maison Caurette. However, as the amount of money owed by the distributor quickly racked up to £150,000 Bilimoria and Reddy felt increas-

Financing Cobra

Estimated Retail Sales in £m

CAGR 40%

Year	Value
1991	0.6
1992	1.3
1993	1.7
1994	2.2
1995	3.3
1996	5.3
1997	7.6
1998	12.8
1999	13.0
2000	19.9
2001	30.9
2002	44.9
2003	52.1
2004	65.3
2005	81.3
2006	96.2

Jul 89
£7K OD

Nov 89
£4K OD

Dec 89
£5K OD

Jul 90 £55K
SFLGS Loan

Jan 92
£50K
Pref
Shares

Feb 93
75% Adv
Factoring

Feb 91
£100K Bills
of Exchange

Oct 93
5% Equity
for £50K

Dec 93
£190
SFLGS
Loan

Oct 94
200K
Conv
Pref
Shares

Dec 95
£50CK
Private
Placement
Sold 23%
Equity

May 96
OD Incr to
£30K

Jun 96
Invoice
Finance
80% Adv

Sep 96
DD £75K
Facility

Dec 97
OD Incr to
£60K

Jan 98
DD £125K
Facility

Jul 98
£100K
Convertible
Pref Shares

Sep 98
NM3 Invoice
Finance 85%
Adv

Nov 98
£750K

Apr 99
OD Incr to
£150K

Aug 99
OD £250K
Facility

Jan 00
Trade
Finance
Facility
£450K UI

Aug 00
DD £350K
Facility

Feb 01
DD £600K
Facility

Jan 02
DD £1.6m
Facility

Oct 02
£400K OD
£1.65m
Loan
£2.5m
Invoice
Finance

Apr 03 £4m
Convertible
Pref Shares

£2m DD
Facility

Aug 04 £1m
Trade
Finance

Sep 04 £5m
Convertible
Pref Shares

Jan 04
£250K
Loan

Oct 05 £7m
Convertible
Pref Shares

£4m Pref
Shares
Redeemed

Jul 06
£25m PIK

£2.5m
Ordinary
Shares

£12m Pref
Shares
Redeemed

37

KARAN'S BUSINESS TIPS: OWNERSHIP

'As your sales are growing, you know the value of your brand is growing. Hold on to those shares as long as you can. I may have started off £20,000 in debt but I still own 67 per cent of Cobra Beer.'

ingly uncomfortable. So after five months of the trial they pulled out. Maison Caurette was sold a few weeks later and the resulting company went into liquidation owing Cobra £60,000 – a debt which fortunately Cobra had insured. At about the same time, Reddy expressed a desire to leave Cobra.

The company needed more money, both to fund future growth as well as the buy-out of Bilimoria's partner Arjun Reddy, who had decided to go his own way. (Bilimoria took on Reddy's share, but assumed his liabilities.)

After consulting with the company's accountants Grant Thornton, he worked out he needed to raise the sizeable sum of £500,000. Bilimoria had borrowed the maximum permitted under the government small firms loan guarantee scheme. There were no significant assets to offer as security against a conventional loan. The last option was to give up some equity. It was something that Bilimoria had resisted until now. Having acquired Reddy's stake, Bilimoria now owned 95 per cent of the company.

But, like any entrepreneur knows, having 100 per cent of the shares in a company that fails because it does not have enough cash to fund growth is pointless. It is far better to know when it is the right time to cede some shares.

'Grant Thornton said you have got to bite the bullet and just do it,' he recalls. The accountants suggested that he give up around 20 per cent of the company in a combination of equity and convertible preference shares, which he might be able to redeem later.

The convertible preference shares offered investors a chance to earn an annual dividend equivalent to 15 per cent of their stake, payable in instalments every six months, for three years. If the company was unable to make one of the six-monthly payments then that payment would roll over to the next payment date. At the end of the three year period the investors could either convert their preference shares into ordinary shares with the right to a normal dividend, if paid, or cash them in for their original value.

In Cobra's case the preference shares were structured in a way that allowed Bilimoria to prevent the conversion into ordinary stock, by the company redeeming the shares and paying a premium dividend. This allowed Bilimoria to avoid diluting his shareholding. With the premium dividend the investor stood to double his original investment.

To make commercial sense the company needed to grow at a rate above the dividend rate to make issuing preference shares, as opposed to ordinary shares, worthwhile. As investors usually prefer to buy ordinary shares Bilimoria needed to use his selling skills

'I had to convince them that the company was worth investing in and that involved being absolutely transparent and open and saying, yes, I could buy them out, but if I buy, they get a very good return,' says Bilimoria. 'I also pointed out that in a downside scenario, preference shares are always paid up before equity shares.' His task was helped by the fact that, even as early as 1995, Cobra was a strong brand that many people recognised.

Cobra's value increased sharply between 1995 and 1998, and Bilimoria exercised his option to buy out all the preference shares and has continued to do so in future issues of preference shares. And, as Cobra has grown more solid and established, the dividend it pays on convertible loan stock has fallen from 15 per cent to 8 per cent, and the total cost to the company including the premium on redemptions from 33 per cent to 12 per cent.

In the end, Bilimoria reached his fundraising target of £500,000 by giving away 23 per cent of his equity. Had he not managed to raise around a third of the cash via convertible preference shares, he would have had to give up around ten per cent more. He has only sold a small amount of shares since and, to this day, he holds 67 per cent of Cobra's stock.

The individuals who bought ordinary shares back in the early 1990s have done very well out of their investment. The biggest single investor in the fundraising round paid £50,000 for five per cent of the company, which at the time was valued – before the £500,000 injection – at £1.5m. Today Cobra is valued at £110m and the value of that investor's stake has risen to £4m. Another investor was Stephen Hacking, whose brother was in Bilimoria's class at school. When he put in £10,000 he told the Cobra founder that 'my children's school fees are in your hands'. He can safely put them down for Eton now: his shares are worth over £500,000.

'It is important to make a distinction here. This is not creative accounting,' Bilimoria says. 'This is about being creative and innovative and keeping a broad perspective on financing methods. My aim is, and always has been, to hold on to my shares, because I know that as the company grows, the brand value is going to grow and the value of my shares is going to grow. If I sell shares then I know I am going to be giving away value and I know it is going to be worth much more looking ahead.'

COBRA COMMENT:
ANUJ CHANDE – FINANCIAL ADVISOR

I have known Karan since 1991, and am one of his key financial advisers. My firm acts as auditors to Cobra Beer Ltd. In the early days (starting when he was operating from his Kings Road flat) I was very heavily involved in helping Karan raise equity and debt funding to help grow his business. At that time his business was turning over just under £1m. Since then I have also been involved in advising on strategy and funding issues, and I believe Karan now regards me as one of his trusted advisors who he will talk to before embarking on any major strategic move.

What makes Cobra special as a business?
The passionate and determined leadership of its founder, who instils enormous inspiration and loyalty in his employees.

What aspect of the Cobra business would you hold up as best practice to other entrepreneurs and business owners?
- *The focus and attention given to the individual development and training of individuals.*
- *The creativity in the development of its products/packaging/advertising.*
- *The courage to follow its convictions and do things that are not conventional (e.g. advertising campaigns, using an Indo British team to do adverts).*
- *The founder enrolling himself on the Cranfield business growth program.*

Could you recall one memory or story of your experiences with Cobra that defines the Karan Bilimoria and Cobra approach to business?
In the early days we had introduced him to a high net worth individual who was willing to invest a substantial amount in the business. However as the transaction progressed and legals were underway it became clear that there was not a meeting of minds and the investor was putting him and his business into a tight corner. Karan, to his credit, turned down the transaction on a matter of principle despite the business needing the funding. This showed the integrity of the man.

I recall another occasion when Cobra's bankers took a very tough stance on the business and sought repayment of some of their facilities almost overnight forcing the business to the brink of bankruptcy. Karan, through the loyalty of his staff to him, managed to raise money from them. In addition, short term financiers who we introduced to him gave him funding, but he was forced to put his own home on the line. This occasion demonstrated very clearly two major traits Karan has – the sheer determination he has in everything he does, and the true loyalty he inspires in others.

TO FLOAT, OR NOT TO FLOAT

Bilimoria is on record as saying that he expects Cobra Beer to float in 2009. This date may shift though. Bilimoria has pushed out plans to list before, as alternative routes to finance became available.

Bilimoria is not adverse to venture capital. It depends on the circumstances. Cobra Beer managed to grow without going down the venture capital route. For other businesses he readily admits that it may be the only option.

It is the same with floating the business. There are a number of reasons why a business might float, he says. One may be because you think that way you will get the best valuation for your company, so that you can raise money to grow the business. Some people float to raise the profile of the company. There are a lot of companies that don't have a high profile, and flotation certainly increases the profile of your company. Neither of these reasons applies to Cobra though, says Bilimoria.

Another reason to float is to offer an exit to existing shareholders, whether they are venture capitalists, institutions or individuals, who want to realise their investment. A flotation also enables you to use your shares as the currency to make acquisitions as part of your future strategy.

A listing on a stock exchange isn't all upside, however. There is the reporting involved; it takes up management time, dealing with the reporting requirement, dealing with regular communications with the analysts – that is also an extra time requirement when you float a company.

Plus there is the corporate governance that the shareholders expect to see in a listed company. In Cobra's case Bilimoria believes the business should be run as if it is a floated company anyway. Not only is it good business practice to implement financial control systems, audit committees, remuneration committees, and appoint non-executive directors, but it makes sense if there is a possibility that at some point in the future you may list.

By raising finance from institutions in the way that Cobra has over the last few years, the company is already comfortable with the aspect of road shows, preparing a prospectus, due diligence, and other preparatory work that will be involved with a listing. And the City is already comfortable with Cobra and Bilimoria.

So when Bilimoria talks about flotation he doesn't talk about the money he is going to raise to fund growth, or about rewarding his early stage investors, or about using his shares to leverage deals; instead he talks about credibility.

'There are a number of reasons why somebody would float,' he says. 'And in our case, I know that being afloat as a company would probably give us additional credibility in a global way, for example, in an international market such as India – being a company listed on the London Stock Exchange would add a lot of credibility to the company.'

KARAN'S BUSINESS TIPS:
LOOK AT IT FROM THE BANK'S PERSPECTIVE

If it takes time to raise finance, especially in the early days, says Bilimoria, it is worth keeping in mind that the attitude of different types of investors is completely different. Try putting yourself in the investor's shoes.

A bank relies on security, because they are often making a very small margin, so it might be borrowing at four per cent and lending at six per cent, so there is only a two per cent margin in it. One bad debt hits the bank very badly – which is why it is overcautious. That is why, in the case of many entrepreneur businesses where there is not any security to offer, and no business track record, it makes it very difficult for banks to finance them using traditional loans and overdrafts.

This was even the case with the government backed loan scheme. Cobra's biggest problem was not the DTI giving the guarantee: it was finding banks willing to lend. From the banks' perspective, they had to demonstrate that they were using the same criteria as if they were making the loan on normal commercial terms, and not relying on the government guarantee. And then banks would also point out that despite the government guarantee, they were still exposed to a significant percentage loss on the non-guaranteed portion.

At the other extreme is an investor like a business angel. In Cobra's case its first business angel put in £50,000 in 1993, and got five per cent of Cobra in return. That individual may have taken some trouble to get his lawyers to do due diligence before he made that investment, but to him that £50,000 was money he could have afforded to lose in minutes, let alone hours. Because he was such a wealthy individual, he was taking a chance – as many business angels do (in this case, a risk worth taking: 12 years on, that £50,000 is worth £4m).

'Of course as the business grows, the entrepreneur can offer more assurance in terms of track record and credibility, and also often in terms of different types of security,' says Bilimoria. 'So when our debtor book grew, we could offer our debtors as security for the factoring and invoice discounting, as our business grew and our stocks grew – we could offer stocks as security.'

Entrepreneurs need to appreciate what it looks like from the other side.

KARAN SAYS:

- Good judgment comes from experience. Experience comes from bad judgment.
- Entrepreneurship is like alchemy, turning lead into gold.
- Where there's a will, there's a way.
- Whenever you are given a task, the first thing is to do it. The second thing is to always do that little bit extra that you were not asked to do. Be innovative, be creative, go the extra mile.
- Know how and know why.
- My father's advice to me: wherever you are in the world, integrate to the best of your abilities but never forget your roots.
- Be proud of and passionate about your product or service.
- You get what you pay for.
- The idea for the beer, like most business ideas, I believe stemmed from being passionate about something on the one hand, and absolutely hating something on the other hand.
- Bilimoria talks about serendipity – making fortunate discoveries by accident. He recalls a professor at Cambridge, Mark de Rond, suggesting that, rather than happenstance, perhaps serendipity is seeing what everyone else sees, and yet thinking what no one else thought.

CHAPTER FOUR

LOOK AFTER YOUR PRODUCT (AND IT WILL LOOK AFTER YOU)

IT'S A MATTER OF TASTE

The year 1996 was an important year for Cobra Beer. Sales doubled within 12 months. Perhaps more significantly, Bilimoria decided to move production to the UK. For someone who was obsessed with the product it was a big step, knowing as he did that such a move could easily jeopardise the reputation of the beer.

The two events were closely connected. As the sales curve hockey-sticked upwards the Mysore Brewery struggled to cope with the surge in demand. The beer began to vary in quality. Worse, consignments arrived late, held up along the tortuous route from India to the UK via Singapore or Colombo.

Although the idea of brewing in the UK was attractive, the commercial risk was considerable. What if the fact that the beer was brewed in India, its authentic Indian nature, was a significant factor in the customer's purchasing decision? In that case the consequences for sales could be disastrous.

Bilimoria needed to know what made people buy Cobra. The only way to find out was to ask the consumers. By the mid 1990s the company exhibited at several trade shows throughout the year, as well as at *The Sunday Times* show in London and the BBC Good Food Show in Birmingham. At these shows Cobra would hand out a survey for customers. This time there was a new section.

'Rank in order of importance, the following four things about Cobra beer:

1   That it is brewed to an authentic Indian recipe
2   That it is a premium lager beer
3   That it is imported from India
4   Its less gassy, extra smooth taste'

Bilimoria even made sure that the order of the four factors was changed to eliminate bias if people went for a straight 1, 2, 3, 4.

The results were not what Bilimoria was expecting. By a significant margin the most important thing to the consumer was the less gassy, extra smooth taste. And by an equally long way the least important thing to the consumer was that Cobra Beer was imported from India. The implication was that, providing Cobra Beer retained its distinctive less gassy, extra smooth taste, it didn't matter where it was brewed; in which case it might as well be brewed in the UK.

Not that the existing supplier, the Mysore Brewery was about to let the business go without a fight. The contract was worth a lot of money, and the brewery was pushing for an extended deal as well as some kind of shared ownership of the brand. As it was Bilimoria's sole supplier he was in a weak bargaining position should production be held up. As a result he decided that he and his business development director, Chris Edgcumbe-Rendle, should find a UK brewer as quickly as possible.

> **KARAN'S BUSINESS TIPS:**
> **MARKET RESEARCH**
> *'We conduct formal market research using the best research companies in the world,' says Bilimoria. 'But I will still use every opportunity I can to do the informal market research, just as we did from day one, with my partner and I standing behind a stall in a consumer trade show.'*

SOURCING SUPPLIERS

There were three options on the table: set up a brewery from scratch; buy a brewery; or hire a brewer to produce Cobra under licence.

Setting up a brewery from scratch entailed huge capital expenditure and was ruled out for that reason. Buying a brewery was more feasible as a number of breweries were on the market at that time. Most of them, however, were designed to produce ale rather than lager and, because Cobra was growing so fast, it would need to buy a brewery with spare capacity, which would be expensive.

With the first two options ruled out only option three remained: hire a brewer to produce Cobra under licence. Then followed the next in a series of choices: should they choose one of the major brewers or an independent? One of the best things about the relationship with Mysore Breweries was exactly that, that there was a relationship. Bilimoria knew both the boss of the brewery and the head brewer very well. The brewer was big enough to be good, but small enough and independent enough for Bilimoria to receive a level of personal attention. With one of the majors, he would never have got that.

After deciding to go down the independent route, Bilimoria, with the help of a consultant, shortlisted three independent regional brewers: the Mansfield Brewery; Hall and Woodhouse in Dorset; and Charles Wells in Bedford. Bilimoria was most impressed by Charles Wells. It had state-of-the-art lager brewing facilities, and a good client track record brewing for brands like Red Stripe and Kirin beer. Kirin even uses rice during the brewing process like Cobra.

'In my experience when it comes to quality the Japanese are more meticulous about quality than any other country in the world, as I discovered on a visit there once,' says Bilimoria. Kirin is one of the biggest beer brands in the world, its facilities are excellent and its standards for quality very exacting. The company even posted its own brewer at the Charles Wells brewery, monitoring the production. If it was good enough for Kirin, it had to be good enough for Cobra – top, top quality. It gave me a lot of reassurance.'

Bilimoria then negotiated the contract, clause by clause, with the company's then managing director John Wells – a former barrister. The process took six months and resulted in what Bilimoria considered a very fair five-year contract. In addition to the standard Cobra bottled lager beer, Charles Wells also signed up to produce Cobra's first draught beer. As the draught market accounts for almost 55 per cent of beer sold (65 per cent in 1997), as well as being the main form of beer sold in Indian restaurants, this was an extremely significant development.

STRIVING FOR PRODUCT PERFECTION

The contract was agreed but there was still plenty to do before production could begin at Bedford. Bilimoria had to go through a process similar to the one he had been through with Dr Cariapa, the Mysore Brewery expert, when developing Cobra bottled beer.

On this occasion he couldn't bring Cariapa over to Charles Wells to help with replicating the recipe for the beer or the Mysore Brewery would find out he was in advanced negotiations with a British brewer and stop production. So the brewery had to rely on Bilimoria's knowledge of the recipe and expertise in brewing to produce a taste-alike product.

The problem was, the new brewery didn't think that replicating the beer was feasible. The brewers said straight away that even if Cobra had the exact recipe, line by line, they wouldn't be able to replicate it. The water was different; the malt was going to be European malt, Cobra used Indian malt; the maize was imported from America, Cobra used Indian maize; the rice was coming from Guyana, Cobra used Indian rice; even the yeast was going to be different. The only thing that matched were the hops, because Bilimoria knew which Bavarian hops the brewery in Mysore used, they could be matched exactly.

Bilimoria, however, was unrelenting in his demands to achieve his idea of perfection, despite resistance from Charles Wells' brewing team. 'They would say, no, no, we have never done this before, while I was trying to produce a product and achieve a texture, and asking them to keep an open mind,' says Bilimoria. 'Many of them did keep an open mind, but there were others in the team who were probably asking themselves whether they needed interfering busybodies who don't know what they were talking about, telling them how to do their job. There was a lot of resistance, but later on the same people said I was right.'

Achieving a taste is not just about the recipe or the equipment, points out Bilimoria. It is about the process, about what happens at each stage. The details matter: when the beer is heated up, for example, and when it is cooled down. How much it is heated up. It took the brewers at Charles Wells, with Bilimoria's help, six attempts to match the taste of the Mysore product. But, by the time they had succeeded, Bilimoria thought they had produced a better product than the original. 'Six brews later we said this was it, we had it,' he says. 'It was delicious and I thought we had matched the taste to the Indian Cobra. In fact, I think we had improved it – it was a touch more refreshing.'

BELIEVE IN YOUR PRODUCT

If you are going to change your product, whether it is an incremental improvement or a wholesale change, it is probably a good idea to tell the customers, even though that might be perceived as a commercial risk. You have to trust the product and trust the consumers. In the case of the new Cobra Beer, for example, although Bilimoria's research said differently, there was always a risk that the fact that the beer was no longer brewed in India would adversely affect sales. On the other hand, Bilimoria truly believed the product was an improvement, and the change of brewers was a positive move.

> **KARAN'S BUSINESS TIPS: THE IMPORTANCE OF BELIEF**
> *'It is essential to have passion and confidence in your product; to believe in your product. After all if the CEO does not have faith in the product what kind of signal does that send out?'*

Rather than playing down the move, Bilimoria decided to take the opportunity to update the Cobra look. New bottles were commissioned from Rockware Glass in Yorkshire – one of the leading glass manufacturers in Europe. The bottle size was switched from 650ml to 660ml, the European-approved size – it was the first 660ml beer bottle manufactured in Britain, although it has since been widely imitated by Cobra's competitors. It was also an example of the relentless innovation revealed in more detail in Chapter Seven.

Perhaps more importantly, the redesign extended to the label. 'We were moving up to world class packaging, so it made sense to take the opportunity to evolve the Cobra logo and branding,' says Bilimoria. The task was handed to Ian Mackie, an in-house designer and former art director with Saatchi & Saatchi in South Africa, who eventually came up with Cobra logo used today.

Bilimoria's conviction was one thing. He was delighted with the new brewer and improved product and branding. Not everyone was happy though. The distributors grumbled that switching production from India was bound to have a catastrophic effect on sales.

To add to the stress of launching what was effectively a new product, Cobra's PR company told Bilimoria that a well known drinks journalist was suggesting the Indian brewed Cobra was far superior to the British version. In the early weeks of production at Charles Wells, stocks of Indian-produced Cobra were available alongside the new product and it was possible to sample both. Potentially, this was a hugely damaging turn of events. If the perception took hold that the UK brewed beer was not up to the standard of the Indian brewed Cobra then sales would really suffer, and consumers might not take the opportunity to try it and find out for themselves.

Bilimoria decided there was only one way to deal with the threat to the new product's success: challenge the journalist concerned to a blind tasting. And so the two men, armed only with their taste buds, squared up to each other across a table at the offices of Cobra's PR company on Oxford Street. On the table were four glasses of beer; two contained Cobra beer brewed in India, and two Cobra beer brewed at Charles Wells in Bedford.

The first task was to identify which of the glasses of beer tasted the same and then divide them into two pairs accordingly. Both the Cobra boss and the journalist did this correctly. Then it was crunch time. Bilimoria asked the journalist which of the two he preferred. The journalist, hedging slightly, said there was not much in it. Both were pretty much the same. But Bilimoria pushed him to make choice which, eventually, he did. Having pointed to the beer he preferred the adjudicator stepped in to reveal which one it was. It was the UK-brewed Cobra. Bilimoria gives the journalist a lot of credit, both for the fact that he agreed to the taste-off, as well as for the fact that he took the result with good grace and later wrote a full-page article in a major newspaper about the event.

PROTECTING DISTRIBUTION

On 11 September 2001, the world suddenly became a more uncertain and dangerous place to live and do business in. The threat of terrorism was a very real one, and with the UK lining up alongside the US in the war against terror, London was on the front line, as it later became all too clear.

Bilimoria began to realise that the business was still vulnerable, both physically and economically. With just the one office in London, and one brew-

COBRA COMMENT:

JIM ROBERTSON – HEAD BREWER AND PRODUCTION DIRECTOR, CHARLES WELLS.

What is your connection with Cobra Beer?
I first met with Karan in the autumn of 1996, when I was production manager at Charles Wells. He came with Chris Rendle for lunch at the brewery with our then MD John Wells. From then on I worked closely with them to formulate a recipe and brewing specification for the Cobra beer to be produced in the UK, along with bottle and label formats. We developed the beer over several months (and brews), until Karan was absolutely sure the product match was spot on and what he wanted. My job was then to make sure all subsequent batches met that standard consistently.

What are the things that make Cobra special as a business?
In my view, the things that have made Cobra and Karan successful lie between Karan's personality and his total commitment to his brand; he always listens and goes out of his way to understand all aspects of the beer and business. I am sure there are other business school type reasons, such as identifying a niche market, having a USP, and tracking the rising popularity of Indian cuisine, but for me it will always be the people part – Karan, Heather, and the senior team at Cobra are just really nice people.

What aspects of the Cobra business would you hold up as particularly instructive as best practice to other entrepreneurs and business owners?
Two points I would highlight to others: the attention to detail (including the boring paperwork stuff) and the ability to listen to sound advice. Other items, such as commitment and passion for the business, tend to feature with most entrepreneurs. Perhaps the extra magic Karan has, is his ability to find and engage high quality advisors for everything he does.

Can you recall an experience related to Cobra that defines the Karan Bilimoria approach to business?
One defining moment was the agreement for our second contract term in June 2002. We completed a long round of hard and detailed negotiations just in time, and Karan wanted to host a small signing ceremony to celebrate where we had moved on to in our first five years. As ever, Karan's diary was busy on the day, and whilst Chris and I met up at the office, he was advising a government committee. We moved on to the chosen venue (Zaika restaurant in Hyde Park, as I remember) and Karan phoned to apologise that he was late, as 'Cherie was running late'. When he arrived of course his charm won us over, after all when someone tells you that they had to cut short the Prime Minister's wife so they didn't keep their brewmaster waiting, it does make you feel kind of special.

We have had many other memorable experiences with Cobra, especially with PR and TV crews, but I am most proud of the beer, and how we have used our brewing skill to support the remarkable growth of Cobra.

ing facility in Bedford, the business was totally reliant on the UK market. What if there was a major fire at the brewing facility, or the UK encountered a lengthy economic downturn?

He knew it was possible to move production from one country to another and maintain product quality. The move from the Mysore Brewery in Bangalore to Charles Wells in Bedford had proved that. But it was a process that took six to nine months to complete. If something happened at Charles Wells that prevented the firm from brewing Cobra Beer, then brands like Kirin and Red Stripe would switch production to their breweries at home in Japan and Jamaica. Yes it would be an inconvenience, but a very temporary one. Cobra would be out of business before it could commence brewing anywhere else.

In the same way, Cobra was vulnerable to a slump in domestic demand. Red Stripe had huge sales in its native Jamaica and was active in other export markets. Kirin could rely on its sales in Japan and elsewhere. Cobra, however, was very much reliant on the UK. Bilimoria realised that urgent action was required. 'We had to do something about it – fast,' says Bilimoria.

It had always been Bilimoria's mission to turn Cobra into a global beer brand. Various distractions had prevented him from focusing on this long-term objective, but now it had his full attention. It was good timing too. Cobra had just won its first major international accolade, a gold medal on its debut at the Monde Selection, the world championships of brewing (see Beer Awards on page 55). So, just at the time the company was looking to go global, it had earned an internationally recognised award for quality and taste.

Once Bilimoria had taken the decision to search for an alternative supplier abroad, his next step was to inform existing brewer Charles Wells, so he called in the company's head brewer, Jim Robertson, for a meeting. 'I explained to Jim what our concerns were, and that, with his knowledge, we were going to start looking for a brewer in Europe because we needed to spread our risks,' he says. 'Jim told me he understood our situation.'

Robertson was right to take the news so calmly. Bilimoria had no intention of brewing draught beer abroad. And with sales of Cobra growing so fast, the chances were that it would make little difference to Charles Wells.

Finding a second brewer in Europe turned out to be a lot tougher than moving production from India to the UK. Initially, Cobra's business development director, Chris Edgcumbe-Rendle took charge of the search. His first stop was a well-known brewery in Belgium. But, while Charles Wells successfully matched the taste of the Indian produced Cobra beer within six months, the Belgians were still struggling to do so a year after trials began.

Bilimoria even took Robertson from Charles Wells over to the Belgian brewery to see whether he could help, but an acceptable brew remained elusive.

Robertson's involvement did have one unexpected benefit, however. At Charles Wells, employees retired at 60. Robertson told Bilimoria that production director Robert Knox had just become eligible for his carriage clock in 2003, and left the company. Knox is one of the most experienced brewers in the world, a man who has produced beer in around 20 different countries. After establishing that Knox was at a loose end, Bilimoria gave him a call and he was soon signed up for Cobra. Knox is now Cobra's technical and production director.

Knox set about finding an alternative to the Belgian brewer. He found his first useful lead within a few weeks. Palm, the largest independent brewer in Belgium, suggested he visit a plant they had set up in Poland a few years earlier. Bilimoria wasn't impressed. 'My initial reaction was that Poland wasn't even on our radar,' he says. 'I mean the Czech Republic, Belgium, they are one of the most famous brewing locations in the world – but Poland?'

Fortunately Bilimoria trusted his advisors, and allowed Knox to persuade him that Browar Belgia, the Polish brewer, was worth a look. 'Robert went across, phoned me up and told me, that I needed to get there as fast as possible. It was, he said, a phenomenal brewery, and I would love it.' Bilimoria still had his doubts but got on a plane the following week – it was May 2003 – and headed for Poland. 'The moment I saw this brewery I said, "Wow". If I was setting up a brewery from scratch, everything in this brewery is what I would put in – state-of-the-art German and Belgian equipment.'

Browar Belgia's story was impressive. Established in Kielce in 1995, in its first four years of operation it took its annual production capacity from 0.4 hectolitres to 1.3 million hectolitres –that's roughly equivalent to 130 Olympic-sized swimming pools. (1 hectolitre = 100 litres; 1 megalitre = 1,000,000 litres = c. 1 Olympic swimming pool). Today it is the fourth largest brewer in Poland. Its turnover mushroomed on the back of sales of Palm, Wojak, Frater and Gingers – a ginger-flavoured beer that took 1.5 per cent of the Polish market in its first six months of production. The brewery has twice won bronze medals at the World Beer Cup and has been a silver medallist at the Polish National Beer Festival.

Not surprisingly, Bilimoria was extremely impressed by what he saw: 'The staff at the brewery were Polish, headed by a young Belgian brewmaster called Koen Cruycke, and they had a fantastic attitude – really professional, really go-getting. So we decided to brew with them and, of course, they were very competitive price-wise. Even after paying all the freight costs to bring the beer into Britain, it is more competitive than producing here.'

Once again it took six attempts to get the taste right, but by December 2003 the Polish brewery was producing cases of Cobra in cans for the first time. The new product was launched at 30,000 ft on a Virgin Atlantic flight from London to Delhi. Today, Cobra has two employees based at Browar Belgia to oversee and monitor production, and its approach has paid off handsomely. Of the 13 medals won by Cobra in 2005 Monde Selection Awards, eight were awarded to Cobra beer brewed in Poland.

ESTABLISHING A REPUTATION

One way of persuading consumers to take your product seriously is to win an international accolade or two. It is a great way of building a product's reputation. Bilimoria entered Cobra beer in the first Monde Selection World Quality Awards in 2001 in Brussels.

The Monde Selection is an independent international institute founded in 1961. Apart from recognising excellence in beer production it has the International Contest of Wines, the World Selection of Food Products and the World Selection of Cosmetic Products and Toiletries. Of all the many international awards schemes for beverages, this is the one that Cobra takes most seriously.

It was an inspired decision. Cobra was awarded a gold medal at the first time of asking and went on to win golds in 2002 and 2003, picking up a special trophy reserved for brands winning gold three years in a row along the way. Bilimoria is particularly proud of this achievement because the only other British brand to pull off such a feat alongside Cobra in 2003 was Johnnie Walker whisky, which earned its golds not for its Red Label product but its premium Black, Gold and Blue Label products.

BEER AWARDS

2001 Monde Selection World Quality Awards: Gold Medal.

2002 Monde Selection World Quality Awards: Gold Medal.

2003 Monde Selection World Quality Awards; Gold Medal; International High Quality Trophy.

2004 Monde Selection World Quality Awards: Grand Gold Medal (2); Gold Medal (4).

2005 Monde Selection World Quality Awards: Grand Gold Medal (2); Gold Medal (9); Silver Medals (2).

2006 Monde Selection World Quality Awards: Grand Gold Medal (1); Gold Medal (11); Silver Medal (5).

CHAPTER FIVE

THE COBRA FAMILY

I n the book *Peak Performance: Business Lessons from the World's Top Sports*, Kevin Roberts, Worldwide CEO of Saatchi & Saatchi, the famous advertising agency, studies a number of highly successful sports teams to discover the secrets of their success, including the All Blacks rugby team, the Australian cricket side and the New York Yankees baseball team. Roberts and his fellow authors discover that the teams that manage to be successful over the long term have a family-like atmosphere.

'The more family-like behaviours and feelings you can incorporate into a company, the more sustainable the growth,' he says. 'And I am not talking about an old-fashioned 1950s paternalistic family. I am talking about today's family which is progressive, demanding, yet sharing. The values are progress, ambition, sacrifice for each other, love – not just respect, sharing, nurture. It is not about team, it is all about family.'

Bilimoria may not have read Robert's book, but he seems to have arrived at a similar conclusion because the idea of the family is at the heart of the Cobra business. It runs through all the company's interactions with people. Advisors, mentors, customers, employees, and associates: they are all part of the Cobra extended family.

GETTING THE RIGHT PEOPLE IN

When Arjun Reddy, Bilimoria's business partner, left Cobra in 1995, Bilimoria began to look for a senior executive to help move the company forward. He might have found someone through an executive search company but, as it turned out, it was through Bilimoria's professional network that he found the person he wanted.

Bilimoria was having dinner with a group of his friends at the Oriental Club in London, when someone mentioned the name of Chris Edgcumbe-Rendle. Rendle, who was brought up in India, and spoke Hindi, was running the Edgcumbe Tea and Coffee Company with his wife, but the consensus was that he would be willing to take on a new challenge.

When Bilimoria met Edgcumbe-Rendle at the Cobra office in the Plaza building on the King's Road, the Cobra boss took an instant liking to him. Edgcumbe-Rendle, however, was reluctant to abandon his business to go and work for Cobra. Not one to take no for an answer, Bilimoria suggested that he join Cobra and still run his business part-time; at the same time he came up with an appealing incentive package. Luckily for Bilimoria the charm offensive worked as Edgcumbe-Rendle agreed to join, going on to become one of the most important members of Bilimoria's management team.

'You never know where you are going to find the right person,' observes Bilimoria. 'It doesn't necessarily have to be through a recruitment agency, and it doesn't have to be through an advert in the *Evening Standard*. We have recruited some of our best people through a wide variety of sources.'

KARAN'S BUSINESS TIPS:
TELLING IT LIKE IT IS

Bilimoria believes in telling it as it is. 'If I am I am not happy with something I will say so, and explain why,' says Bilimoria. 'People have got to know where they stand.

'There is no point in treading on eggshells around it – they have got to know you are not happy. On the other hand, if you are happy with something, you must acknowledge it, and I always do it as publicly as possible. Praising someone in front of everybody gives a lot of confidence and pride, it links into everyone having a pride in the organisation – being proud to be part of Cobra, being proud of Cobra – and that is the leader's job again, to ensure that sense of pride.'

WILL – NOT SKILL

As well as having a very open approach to finding staff Bilimoria has very clear ideas about hiring criteria.

Take the example of Cobra's star salesman, now the company's sales director, who joined the company in early 1993. After two years of making do with salesmen working on a commission-only basis, the decision was taken to hire some full-time professionals. An advert was duly placed in the *Evening Standard*. Bilimoria expected some interest, but, given the Cobra brand's limited exposure at the time, he was amazed when the company received over 100 replies.

After interviewing the most promising candidates, Bilimoria and Reddy decided to hire their two top listed candidates. But they had not bargained for the dogged persistence of third placed candidate, Samson Sohail, who wouldn't take no for an answer. A Pakistani Christian who had been granted political asylum, on the face of it Sohail didn't seem a promising candidate. He was working in an off-licence, rather than a sales office, and his English was terrible. Yet his attitude made a positive impression on Reddy and Bilimoria.

Sohail begged to be given a chance to prove himself on a commission-only basis. He asked what target Bilimoria has set the two salesmen already hired. When he was told it was 100 cases of Cobra in four weeks, Sohail said he would do the same in half the time and was so insistent that Bilimoria eventually gave in. Sohail achieved the target inside two weeks. He got his job.

The qualities that got him hired are clear from a story Bilimoria likes to tell. In 1993 Bilimoria's apartment doubled up as the Cobra offices, as well as

> **KARAN'S BUSINESS TIPS: BAD EGGS**
>
> *One 'bad egg' can ruin everything, says Bilimoria. If there is somebody who is unhappy in the company, somebody who is – for whatever reason – disgruntled, that sentiment can spread very quickly. Bilimoria believes in nipping that in the bud straight away. 'If you have an open environment, you get to hear that pretty quickly,' says Bilimoria. 'Deal with that situation immediately, find out what is causing it, and if you can't solve it, the best thing is for that person to leave. Because it affects everyone and it spreads very quickly and it happens on rare occasions, but I have realised that when … you spot a bad egg very, very quickly, you deal with it – otherwise it can ruin everything.'*

the family home. Bilimoria vividly recalls one evening in May 1993, when he and his wife Heather were getting ready to go out for dinner. The couple stepped in to the sitting room for a moment before leaving the apartment and there was Sohail on the phone in the sitting room. It was 9pm. Surprised, Bilimoria remarked on the time and suggested he went home. Undeterred, Sohail continued to make calls, pausing only briefly to tell Bilimoria that he was on call 26 of a target he had set himself of 30 effective calls for the evening. He offered to let himself out after call number 30.

Sohail continued to go from strength to strength. He is now Cobra's sales director, owns a number of properties, earns a significant salary, and has share options worth seven figures. He has also helped to steer Cobra through a period of rapid growth, and from a small company with a predominantly domestic market to a company with significant global sales. Yet if Bilimoria had been hiring along conventional lines, based on qualification, exams, certificates, even previous sales experience, he would have missed out on a valuable member of his executive team.

'We always, always hire for will rather than skill,' says Bilimoria. 'It is the attitude that matters. Obviously, if you find will *and* skill, it is great, but the will is more important than the skill, and we always look for that. Qualifications are not as important as a person's attitude.'

KARAN'S BUSINESS TIPS:
THE ROLE OF THE CEO

CEOs have a tough job to do. But just what should the role of the CEO involve? Bilimoria identifies a number of aspects of the job that he believes are critical to doing it well.

- **Leadership:** As a CEO, says Bilimoria, leadership is absolutely key. As the leader of the company, your role is to inspire, to motivate, to drive forward the whole company.
- **All round skills:** Bilimoria believes that the more of an all rounder you are, the better. In some companies it is traditional for an engineer to always get to the top, in other companies it always the finance person who makes it to CEO. In Bilimoria's case, he is competent enough in all the important

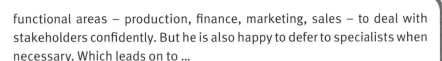

functional areas – production, finance, marketing, sales – to deal with stakeholders confidently. But he is also happy to defer to specialists when necessary. Which leads on to …

- **Team building**: It is the CEOs job to build a team of the people who are the best at what they are doing, get them to work together and get that same level of integration throughout the company.
- **Delegate**: Once you have assembled a team that you trust, you need to create the right organisational atmosphere and culture to allow them to get on with things. But you must also monitor and follow up.
- **Communicate:** As a chief executive, you should be constantly communicating with your team, regardless of where you are in the world. And it is also about coming up with ideas and feeding them through to the team, so they know that although they've been allowed to get on with things, you are still very much engaged as well: it is not a question of, oh well, I'll see you at the weekly management meeting and I don't want to hear from you until then.
- **Getting the balance right between detail and overview:** As well as the regular formal reporting, Bilimoria gets minutes of meetings that are taking place within the company. He also goes through all the reports from the subsidiaries and the different countries, providing feedback where required. In this way he can make sure that he is aware of everything that is going on, so if a figure doesn't look right, he will pick up on it. And it is that attention to detail which is absolutely crucial, combined with being able to stand back and take a sort of strategic overview.
- **Vision:** The chief executive, says Bilimoria, has got to have a vision, to display a certain confidence to show that they are somebody who is looking ahead, who knows where they are going and where the company is going and they have that confidence and the faith that inspires others to go with them on that journey.

RISING THROUGH THE RANKS

Recruiting good staff is just part of the HR process, however. Once you have hired the right people you need to make sure they remain motivated, that they are able to contribute, and that they continue to develop.

Another defining characteristic of Bilimoria's family approach is a willing-ness to promote from within. If they prove that they merit it, then Bilimoria is happy to give people as much responsibility as they can handle at Cobra. Many companies claim to promote from within the organisation accord-ing to ability, but how many companies just pay lip service to the notion? How many companies would push the policy as far as Bilimoria has done at Cobra?

At the Munster Road premises in 1999, a young South African girl used to come by on a bicycle with a sandwich basket and sell sandwiches to the Cobra staff. After a few weeks, one of the Cobra team suggested that she might like to earn some extra money working at Cobra. Accepting the offer she sold sandwiches during the day, and in the evenings came to work at Cobra in telesales.

The girl was so good at telesales that she was offered a full-time job and so gave up selling sandwiches and joined Cobra. Within a year she was telesales manager, in charge of a team of seven people. When Bilimoria's personal assistant left suddenly in 2002, she became PA to the chief executive of the company.

Between 2002 and 2005 she helped build the chief executive's team up to six people. Then, with the company in a period of rapid growth, she was promoted to head of HR; from sandwich girl to head of HR at one of the UK's fastest growing companies in just seven years. 'It gives me so much satisfac-tion to think that you can create an atmosphere in a company where some-body can get from anywhere to anywhere,' says Bilimoria.

LEAVING THE NEST

Ensuring the company is run with a family spirit is not just about how you treat employees when they are with the company. It is also about how you treat them when they decide to move on.

In football, when it comes to dealing with players who want to move on, managers seem to fall into two camps. Some fall out with the player, accuse them of being disloyal, and end up with an acrimonious split. Others recog-nise that players have ambition and a desire to better themselves, and that they may wish to move on to new challenges, and they part on good terms (providing an appropriate transfer fee is arranged, of course).

It is much the same with business. If a CEO loses a rising star in the company, or a long standing member of the firm, because that person wants to move on to a new challenge, the CEO may take it as a personal slight. Things end up turning nasty. Bilimoria is not one of those chief executives, however. If at all possible, he tries to maintain a good relationship with team members who move elsewhere, and, although it is in his nature to do so, it is also good business practice, as events at Cobra have shown.

When Cobra diversified its brewing capabilities in 2003, it found an excellent brewing partner, Browar Belgia, based in Poland. While this was great news for the company, the search for a brewer in Europe did have one hitch. Chris Edgcumbe-Rendle, who was instrumental in helping to find the new brewer, also found a new job in the process.

One of the brewers that Edgcumbe-Rendle had looked at in the Czech Republic was owned by an Englishman with ambitious plans to create a new beer brand and turn it into a global contender. He wanted Edgcumbe-Rendle to be managing director of the new venture.

In the six years since his name had come up over dinner at the Oriental Club, Edgcumbe-Rendle had become one of Bilimoria's most trusted executives. Bilimoria had gone to some lengths to get him to accept the job in the first place. Now the Cobra founder set out to persuade Edgcumbe-Rendle to stay on.

The new job offer was extremely tempting. Apart from the challenge of helping create a new beer, and a good salary, Edgcumbe-Rendle was offered 20 per cent of the company.

Bilimoria refused to be beaten. He explained that the company was going places, it was going to float, and Edgcumbe-Rendle had a great future with Cobra. He also reminded Edgcumbe-Rendle that Cobra's share option scheme was soon to be put in place, pointing out at the same time that while Cobra was a proven success, with the new venture, 20 per cent of nothing was nothing.

Edgcumbe-Rendle, however, was adamant. It was an opportunity to run a company and he was not about to let it go. Bilimoria accepted his decision with good grace. 'Our staff turnover rate is very low,' he says, 'but when people leave over the years for whatever reason, we always accept that. We like them to leave on good terms, on happy terms, and invariably we keep in touch with people who have left.'

And to show there are no hard feelings, there is even a company policy where the person leaving is given a month's salary for every year worked in the company as a thank you, even if the person is leaving voluntarily. Edgcumbe-Rendle, who had been with the company for six years by this time, was given half a year's pay when he left, as well as a lavish and emotional leaving party.

It was not long, however, before he was back. About nine months later Bilimoria received a call from him. 'How was he getting on?' inquired his old boss. 'Not very well,' replied Edgcumbe-Rendle. It was, according to Edgcumbe-Rendle, boring and dull. In fact he hated it there and missed the buzz at Cobra, the family atmosphere, the team. It was dreadful. Could he come back? Of course he could, Bilimoria said.

Bilimoria spoke to his executive team, and Edgcumbe-Rendle returned to the job he loved. He didn't go straight back on the main board, but a year later, in 2004, he rejoined the board and it was as if the whole episode had never happened.

'What this shows is how important the culture and atmosphere of a company is,' says Bilimoria. 'It is so easy to take it for granted, and think the grass is greener on the other side. So always try to leave on good terms because you never know when you might be back in contact.'

THE IMPORTANCE OF ADVISORS

Mentors are an often overlooked part of many a CEO and corporate success story. The contribution that mentors have played in the Cobra business should not be underestimated. Without the mentors there probably would be no Cobra Beer.

At critical moments in the company's history, external advice and encouragement has been instrumental in moving the company forward. It might be something as apparently insignificant as the words of encouragement Bilimoria received from his mother's cousin during a lunch in a Chinese res-

THE COBRA ENTREPRENEURS

Not all the Cobra people who leave return like Rendle did. But it is a credit to Bilimoria's willingness to nurture talent, promote within, and give responsibility to his staff that many of his employees have been extremely successful in their life after Cobra.

Julia Minchin is just one example. In 1995, shortly after Cobra had moved in to new premises in the King's Road in Chelsea, London, Bilimoria hired Minchin who was one of his wife's best friends. She had worked for a string of distinguished employers in the past, including at Buckingham Palace in the Lord Chamberlain's office, and while she joined as Bilimoria's PA and office manager, she soon assumed a wider role as the company's first marketing manager.

'She was brilliant,' he says, 'I mean absolutely superb – and the beauty of it all was, that she actually grew with us.'

When she left Cobra she started up the highly successful children's clothing and accessories company, Hippy Chick; one of a number of Cobra alumni who went on to become entrepreneurs in their own right.

Others include salesman, Jewel Zaman, who left to start his own restaurant and distributor, and Alex Klaus who started a vodka and beer importing business.

taurant off Gerrard Street in London's Chinatown, at a point when Bilimoria was having serious doubts about the decision to run his own business: 'Don't be worried that you are doing so many different things. One day one of them will be big. You should just stick with it.'

Another mentor of Bilimoria's was Arjun Reddy's uncle, Keshow Reddy. Bilimoria describes him as a 'godfather figure', a man whose judgment he trusted and whose advice he valued. In the early days, when the two young entrepreneurs were importing various goods into the UK before the beer business, they would visit the man they called Uncle Keshow at least once a month and talk through their business problems. He would give advice and do his best to introduce them to people who might be useful contacts.

It was at one of these meetings that they told Uncle Keshow they planned to import Indian seafood. Much to their surprise Uncle Keshow said that one of his friends ran a seafood exporting company in Cochin in South India.

KARAN'S BUSINESS TIPS:
INTEGRATE YOUR ADVISORS

External advisers should be treated as members of the corporate family, says Bilimoria.

'Our AGMs are better attended than a lot of plc AGMs,' he points out. 'I remember the chief executive of Joshua, our advertising agency, said, "Do you know Karan, I've got to admit something. I've been in the advertising industry for years, but this is the first client AGM I have ever been invited to and that I have ever attended." And next to him was Richard Williams, who is one of the gurus of the design world, and head of one of the most award-winning design agencies in the country. He said, "That makes two of us. I have never been to a client AGM before".

'By creating that atmosphere you make them part of your team. Relate to them very openly and it will help drive creativity. When we deal with packaging agencies, design agencies and advertising agencies, we don't just give them a brief and say, "Thank you very much", and then either accept or reject what they produce. We work with them.'

He had just returned to India the day before, after a business trip to England, and he had left some brochures for the seafood division with Uncle Keshow, saying if anyone was interested to let them know.

After an unsuccessful search for the relevant brochure, he promised to send it to them when it turned up. It duly arrived and, after looking through it, Bilimoria noticed the line on the final page that said: 'Pals Seafood is a division of Mysore breweries. Brewers of the famous Pals Beer.'

Bilimoria recognised the Pals beer brand. The company used to supply the defence services in India with lots of beer. It was one of the most popular beers in the Indian Army messes. At once Bilimoria saw a way to develop his beer idea. 'I told Arjun, my partner, to forget importing seafood. This is my beer idea. I know Pals beer. Let's ask them if they are interested in exporting some beer'.

Uncle Keshow promptly received a phone call explaining that the two entrepreneurs had decided not to go into the seafood importing business, but they wanted to import beer instead. Fortunately for them, the owner of Pals was a personal friend of their mentor and, after being contacted by

KARAN'S BUSINESS TIPS: DON'T UNDERESTIMATE THE VALUE OF FRIENDS AND FAMILY.

Friends and family can be an invaluable source of help and advice. Some of the most useful advice Bilimoria ever got was from his father. It was the summer of 1982 and Bilimoria was on his holidays in India, just before he started his first 'proper' job at accounting firm Arthur Young, now Ernst & Young. His father had just become a Major General in the Indian Army and was commanding a mountain division on the border with China. The young Bilimoria turned up at his father's office, after making an appointment with his father's aide-de-camp, to ask his advice.

Bilimoria vividly remembers entering his father's vast office and the advice he received there. 'Son, you are starting at the bottom,' said Bilimoria's father. You will be given lots of tasks. The first thing when you are given a task is do it. The second thing is do that little bit extra that you are not asked to do.'

It is some of the best advice he has ever been given, Bilimoria says, because what it meant was: 'Always take the initiative, always be creative, always be innovative and always go that extra mile'. And that is what it is really all about – going that extra mile.

Uncle Keshow, he called back straight away to say he was very keen on the idea. Cobra Beer was underway.

EXTENDED FAMILY

It is not just employees who are part of Cobra's extended family. Business advisors are treated in the same way. Accountants, bankers, ad agencies, brewers, suppliers, customers; Bilimoria sees them all as part of the Cobra clan. He expects them to share the Cobra values in terms of respect and trust; in a way he treats them as he would his employees, and if they fall short of his expectations in this regard he is not afraid to move on. To those advisors that fit well into the Cobra family, Bilimoria is fiercely loyal.

Often, Bilimoria sources his advisors through his existing business network. For example, when he was looking for a banker that would lend him £195,000 as part of a government-backed enterprise loan, he was referred to someone at the Midland (now HSBC) by Grant Thornton, his accountants.

When Bilimoria visited the banker who was in charge of the Ealing branch, he knew almost immediately that he had found someone he could work with over the long-term. 'I remember he was an amazing guy, called Andrei Warhaftig. He said: "I believe in you, I believe in your brand, and I trust you".'

On the other hand Bilimoria will not hesitate to move his business if he feels that Cobra values like trust and respect are not reciprocated.

Towards the end of 1995, Cobra experienced a cash-flow crisis. The ordinary and preference share issue exercise to raise £500,000 had taken five months to complete and the wait stretched the company's financial position almost to breaking point. At the point when Bilimoria needed the support of his existing bank the most, the bank let him down. Warhaftig had retired and Bilimoria did not enjoy the same kind of relationship with his new manager at the bank.

Despite the fact that Bilimoria had kept his new bank manager fully briefed on the progress of the share issue, and pleaded with him to be understanding about the occasional breach of the company's overdraft limit, the new man was inflexible.

'He bounced one of our cheques,' recalls Bilimoria bitterly. 'He didn't trust me, even though I kept him fully in the picture. And sure enough that money came in the next day. He caused me a huge embarrassment by bouncing that cheque.' Bilimoria told him that the moment the share issue was concluded, he would be moving Cobra's business. And, true to his word, he moved as soon as he could.

'I will never forget that moment,' reflects Bilimoria. 'In the same way that I will never forget people who have helped me, I will never forget people who have let me down, who have not trusted me. That is all this boils down to.'

And that is another cornerstone to Bilimoria's business dealings – trust. It may require you to be a good judge of character, and maybe to believe the

KARAN'S BUSINESS TIPS:
TRUST AND A HANDSHAKE

In Bilimoria's world business means trust, and trust means that you really can do business on a handshake. Bilimoria points to his relationship with Gandhi Foods with whom he has built up a considerable trust over the years.

'To this day, sometimes when Mr Gandhi wants a huge amount of beer or if we want some cash very quickly, he will sign a cheque for £500,000 without a contract – forget a contract – without any beer, without any delivery notes, just on trust.

'The more I think about it, looking back, so much of it is down to trust. It is down to Mr Balan – the owner of the brewery in Bangalore – believing in me and trusting in me, the fact that he lent me the money to buy the first container from him, that he would introduce me to friends of his abroad, who would give us unsecured loans purely on his name and his recommendation because he trusted us. It is trust, trust, trust – all the way. I was at the races in Bangalore with Mr Balan and a business acquaintance of his. We were watching a race and I was introduced to his acquaintance who said to me: "Young man, remember. Empires are built on trust" I will never forget that.'

best of people, rather than the worst, but ultimately trust underpins all good business relationships.

When Bilimoria met his new banker at Coutts for the first time, the banker explained how he trusted Bilimoria. He also explained that, on the whole, he trusted people in general. That attitude had served him well, because, as a senior banker, in all his years of experience he had only been let down by three individuals, all of whom were conmen.

PARTING WAYS

Not all professional relationships work out. Many run a natural course and then a company just outgrows its advisors. Whatever the reason, it makes good business sense to demonstrate some dignity and respect when parting ways with business stakeholders, whether they are advisors, suppliers even customers.

For example, Cobra moved its advertising from Saatchi's to McCann Erickson in 2003. Not because the Cobra team had fallen out with Saatchi, but because Bilimoria wanted fresh creative input. 'We parted as friends, because we really liked them and they really liked us. We respected them, they respected us,' says Bilimoria. 'That mutual respect is very important in any relationship, whether it is a husband and wife, or whether it is with business colleagues or clients and advisors. When we left, we left with the door open and sure enough, with McCann Erickson it worked out for a while, but then we wanted to go back to Saatchi's, and because we had left that door open, we could go back to them.'

To this day, Mike Parker at Saatchi and Bilimoria have a very good relationship. Although not clients of the agency any longer, the two speak on the phone regularly. And you never know when they might work together again.

Another example is Close Invoice Finance, an invoice discounting company that Bilimoria used and one of the best companies Bilimoria has worked with in this area.

Bilimoria was particularly impressed with the service he got. The firm really tried to look after its customers and trusted them. The managing director came out every year to visit Cobra and have lunch with Bilimoria and give his personal advice. It was like a management consultant coming and giving great advice as an added service.

'When we eventually outgrew them, we didn't fall out with them,' says Bilimoria. 'They insisted on taking us out to lunch to say, "Look, we've appreciated you as a client and we wish you all the best for your future and we really thank you for the business you have given us and we understand you have to move on because you are growing and you need to".

'If you part with people in a business relationship, always do it amicably because you never know when your paths may cross again. It is always, always good to do that.'

THE COBRA BUZZ

A good way of finding out just what kind of organisational culture a business has is to pay a visit to the headquarters. It doesn't matter what the values that are hanging on the wall say. They can proclaim that a company is a fun place to work in huge capital letters, but if the employees are wandering around with a miserable look fixed on their face, it probably isn't. It may claim to be an egalitarian, participative work environment, but if the senior management is safely secreted in plush office accommodation on the 15th floor while the minions mill around in cubicles downstairs, if the boss dines in the executive restaurant while the staff eat in the cafeteria, it probably isn't. The website may say empowerment; the form filling may scream hierarchical bureaucracy.

> **KARAN'S BUSINESS TIPS: GIVING ORDERS**
>
> *'You certainly can't order people around,' says Bilimoria. 'It's got to be that people just love what they are doing, know they have got the freedom to get on with things, know that they are appreciated, know that they are part of the whole organisation – the whole family – and also have confidence in their leader. Because in a corporate environment, where people don't like it, they leave.'*

One visit to Cobra's headquarters, around the corner from Parsons Green in London, and you know immediately what kind of company you are dealing with. For a start everyone looks happy – busy, but happy. The offices are open plan and there is constant interaction between the people working there. What about the plush boss' office on the 15th floor? Not a chance. Bilimoria's office is feet away from the rest of his employees, and the door is usually open.

Right there and then you get a sense of what Cobra is about as an organisation: fun tempered with professionalism. 'It has got to be fun,' says Bilimoria. 'There is absolutely no point otherwise. You have got to enjoy what you are doing, and you have got to enjoy the people you are with. You create an atmosphere where you can see that everyone just gets on, and gets on well, and both they and you can feel it.

The company organises a number of social events for the employees. Appropriately, there is the family day, which traditionally takes place in

Sussex, at the farmhouse of one of the directors. Everyone drives down and spends the whole Saturday there. Various activities are arranged for the children. There might be rock climbing, trampolines, cricket, bucking broncos, laser shooting, football. Bilimoria still has the photo of the first Cobra Family Day, which took place in 2000. There are about 20 people in the photograph. In the 2006 photo there are 200.

Then there are the impromptu celebrations. After Bilimoria was formally introduced to the House of Lords in July 2006, he returned to the office at the end of the afternoon, and took the entire office out for a drink at the pub on the green nearby. After which, Bilimoria and the Cobra team went for a curry and a few Cobra beers no doubt.

Make no mistake: employees know when you are faking it. Bilimoria really does care about his people. 'It was one of the most important days of my life, I was with my family in the afternoon; and then in the evening I wanted to be with my team.'

Bilimoria makes sure that the employees' achievements are acknowledged and celebrated too. The office meet on a Friday at what Bilimoria calls his Friday gather-round. It is then that the sales figures are announced but also people are recognised and rewarded for all kinds of achievements. It might be recognising the individuals who helped make the company's Golf Day so outstanding, and just applauding them. Birthday cards are presented, usually accompanied by a bottle of champagne or a gift token. Bilimoria signs all the birthday cards for his employees, whatever country they are based in.

Don't get the idea that Bilimoria is a soft touch though. The organisational culture is about balance. When you have got a family atmosphere, an informal atmosphere, an open atmosphere – it must be counterbalanced by always being professional.

'We have got a wonderful atmosphere here but you must always remember that things have to be professional, and follow best practice. So we have got Investors in People accreditation, we make *The Sunday Times* "Best Companies to Work For" list. We are accredited under the star system,' he says.

'With an in-house consultant we have in-house HR advice on a very professional basis, to ensure that we have all the proper procedures – interview processes, induction processes, mentoring, assessments, all that. Entrepreneurs need to remember that the business should be as professional as any large organisation.'

KARAN'S BUSINESS TIPS:
DIVERSITY

Bilimoria is convinced that diversity in an organisation is a huge competitive advantage. He was a member of a Department of Trade and Industry sponsored taskforce, headed up by Laura Tyson, who was Dean of London Business School, which looked at the issue of diversity on boards.

The taskforce investigated the effect of board diversity in organisations and concluded that the more diverse boards tended to be more effective. Diversity brought in a huge variety of different approaches, and, most importantly, a diversity of mindset. It enriches any decision-making process.

The Cobra boss sometimes refers to his management team as a mini United Nations, and there is diversity across the spectrum, from age to expertise, from faith to country of origin. That diversity is reflected throughout the Cobra organisation.

'In Cobra, we have over twenty different nationalities represented, people from Spain, Poland, India, Pakistan, Bangladesh, Sri Lanka, South Africa, Kenya, Canada ... people from all over the world,' says Bilimoria. 'It is so enriching, because it creates a balance and you have got this huge variety of backgrounds and approaches and mindsets and they all come together in this ... and I just think it is this huge advantage to have.'

COBRA COMMENT:
JAMIE BERGER – NON-EXEC DIRECTOR OF COBRA

I met Karan when I was an undergraduate at Cambridge in 1987. He rapidly became one of my closest friends. I had a house as an undergraduate which I sold shortly after coming down and put the money behind Karan on the basis that he'd lose my money more slowly than I would. Not only that, but he had a wonderful idea, the genesis of which I had lived, and was a qualified accountant so knew what he was doing financially.

I have thus been part of Cobra from the days when the company didn't even have a name. Many were the evenings that I sat in the flat Karan shared with Arjun in the Fulham Palace Road tasting beers from India and comparing them to European ones to get the taste right.

Partly on the basis of my investment, and partly because of my interest and enthusiasm about the product, Karan asked me to become a director in 1995. It has been the best education in business that I could ever have hoped for. Karan and I have remained very close and there has never been any problem at all about the mixing of business and friendship.

I trust Karan implicitly, and I think that his integrity and loyalty are two of his finest qualities and cannot but have contributed in no small way to his success.

What makes Cobra special as a business?
I think that it is in largely due to the fact that the company is an extension of Karan: its values and ideals being his – the emphasis on integrity ('to aspire and achieve against all odds, with integrity') is a cornerstone of his personality and the way he interacts with others.

What aspect of the Cobra business would you hold up as best practice to other entrepreneurs and business owners?
The company has an extraordinary culture about it – if you have spent any time in the office you cannot but understand what I mean. But it is more than culture alone, there is something of a family about it – I often talk of the 'Cobra Family.'

In business there are so few people who can match Karan for his honesty, consideration and generosity, and business is the poorer for it. On the subject of generosity, I remember Karan telling me proudly about the number of people who are putting their children through private education as a result of their Cobra earnings, and the fact that he wanted to make Samson, one of the longest-serving employees, a millionaire – which he now is!

CHAPTER SIX

'MY NAME IS DAVE, AND I'M A CURRYHOLIC'

Cobra's commitment to sales and marketing is vividly illustrated by the number of staff it employs to handle those two functions. There are close to 150 people employed in four countries at the end of 2006, of which 30 per cent are involved in sales and 10 per cent in marketing and PR. That means that these two functions account for almost half of the company's head-count. It hasn't always been that way though.

GIVING SALES A PUSH START

A car called Albert (*pr.* Al-bear) played a key role in the transformation of Cobra beer from an idea into a genuine business. It was the nickname of the company's first delivery vehicle, the Citroen 2CV that Bilimoria was driving at the time.

'I brought it for £295, with money I borrowed from Arjun,' recalls Bilimoria. 'It could carry exactly fifteen cases of Cobra beer. You could see the road through the floor of the car. Most days it required a push start. Eventually it failed its MOT three times.'

While the competitors' beer was distributed in vans furnished with smart corporate livery, consignments of Cobra were transported around in an old, battered, bright green, bottom-of-the-range Citroen.

When the first consignment of Cobra arrived in the UK, the distributors in the UK subjected the beer to a haze test, designed to establish whether the beer was of good enough quality to be sent to customers. Although it was within the legal parameters, it failed to meet the distributors' requirements. Now there was a consignment of beer, a bill, but no distributors. They needed to find a replacement distributor but until that happened there was only one solution: Bilimoria and Reddy would have to shift some beer. And it wasn't going to be easy.

By the time Cobra entered the market, Carlsberg was well-established as the number one lager brand in Indian restaurants. Two others, Dortmund Union, distributed by the German Lager Company, and Kingfisher, which had been active in the market for eight years by now, were doing well. Worse, Cobra was up against a number of other Indian beers attempting to break into the British market at that time. Golden Eagle, one of India's biggest beer brands, was exporting stock to the British market, as was Bombay brewer Maharaja, the producer of Bombay pilsner, and others.

In the face of such tough competition, the owners of a fledgling brand that was only available in double-sized bottles, and which had no marketing budget to speak of, met with nothing but scepticism from distributors. Bilimoria recalls: 'I remember having a meeting with one of the biggest distributors who said, "Sorry, we've got our own Indian beer which we are going to make a success of, and anyway, yours isn't going to work".'

Bilimoria and Reddy were forced to sell directly to the restaurants themselves. So they developed a low-budget sales and marketing strategy geared to making Cobra a premium brand. 'We decided to go for the best restaurants first,' says Bilimoria. 'If the best restaurants stocked the product, we could use them as a reference when we went to other restaurants. We could say, "Look, if it's good enough for them, it should be good enough for everyone".'

The way they found those first few customers is a good example of some selling basics: using your personal network for sales leads and introductions; tenacity and a willingness to put in the long hours; and being highly tuned to the needs of the customer.

Bilimoria contacted a former military attaché with the Indian High Commission in London, who had since returned to India. During his posting Bilimoria's contact had eaten at a number of Indian restaurants on a regular

basis. Bilimoria persuaded him to write to the owners of the Indian restaurants he used to eat at in London, and ask them to let Bilimoria come in and
speak to them about Cobra.

Timing was also important. They found that the lunchtime period was
the best time to make sales calls as the restaurants were likely to be less busy
than in the evenings. Bilimoria once succeeded in visiting 13 restaurants in
one lunchtime.

Even when he managed to get in front of the restaurant owners Cobra
was not an easy sell. For a start Cobra was £1 a case more expensive than the
opposition, and Bilimoria always insisted that the minimum order was five
cases. And then there was the size of the bottle. The restaurant owners were
used to small 330ml bottles or draught beer, and would baulk at Cobra's
much larger 650ml bottles.

But Bilimoria soon learnt how to counter these objections effectively.
'People would say, "You have something unknown, more expensive, and
you are saying I have to take five cases?",' he recalls. 'In response, we would
say, "Look, the secret of this product's success is in its smoothness and its
drinkability. The reality is, because it is smoother your customers will eat
more and, if they want to, they will drink more. If they drink more, you make
more. You are going to make more profit. So forget about the £1 additional
cost, because we are going to make you many pounds more profit".'

To counter the objection about the bottle size Bilimoria came up with a
sharing concept. Instead of ordering a bottle each, diners would share the
larger sized Cobra bottle. 'People ended up consuming more because they
were sharing; it created a much better atmosphere,' observes Bilimoria.
'People on neighbouring tables could not figure it out. They saw these
large bottles, but they weren't wine bottles, so what were they? Usually
they would ask to try one and Cobra drinking would spread like wildfire
around the restaurant. To this day over half of our sales are in the big bottle
size.'

To emphasise how it is possible to succeed in even the toughest selling
environments it is worth mentioning that two thirds of Britain's 'Indian'
restaurants are owned by Bangladeshi Muslims who don't drink for religious
reasons. Bilimoria would launch into his patter about how his product was
the best Indian beer around, extra smooth and less gassy, offer to let the

owners try it, only to be told that they did not drink. However, the restaurant owners taught Bilimoria one of his first lessons in business: to put the customer first. They said, 'it doesn't matter that we don't drink, it's the customers who matter. If our regular customers like it we'll place our first order, and if the rest of our customers like it we'll re-order.' Bilimoria and Reddy would leave a few bottles for a restaurant's regulars to sample, with a promise that if the customers liked it then the restaurant would place an order – and they invariably did. Given this chance, the product had to deliver – and it did.

To this day Bilimoria always says he will never forget what the Indian restaurants did for him by giving him a chance, and will always be grateful for their support.

SPEAKING THE CUSTOMER'S LANGUAGE

Another key part of the company's sales success early on, was knowing when to expand the sales team, and who to recruit. One important addition to the team was the wife of one of Bilimoria's friends, who was half-Bengali and half English. With the advantage of speaking fluent Bengali she proved particularly successful selling to the Bangladeshi restaurateurs who formed the biggest single grouping in a sector that also included Pakistanis, Sri Lankans, Nepalese, and, of course, Indians.

Bilimoria understood the importance of connecting with the customer in order to develop an ongoing relationship. With so few people involved in the nascent operation, there was a temptation to neglect follow-up service. Bilimoria might be thousands of miles away in India dealing with various production glitches while an overworked Reddy tried to keep the sales momentum going at home. In such circumstances, it was easy to let customer care standards slip.

'Sometimes I would call someone who had not reordered, who would say, "You didn't phone me. Why didn't you phone me? I ran out of the beer last

> **KARAN'S BUSINESS TIPS: THE 7PS (OR 6PS AND 1F)**
> *Marketing guru Philip Kotler famously has his 4Ps of marketing: product, price, promotion, and place. Bilimoria prefers to talk about his 7Ps. They are: product, price, promotion, place, then people and passion, and finally finance, or phinance, as he puts it.*

week and, of course, if you had phoned, I would have asked for more. Please send it. Please bill it to me today",' says Bilimoria.

Most Indian restaurants are owner-managed with a small team of people that includes chefs and waiters. Apart from attending to customers, the manager has to deal with all the supply issues that come with preparing fresh food daily. His roster of suppliers could run into the dozens, ranging from butchers and dry food suppliers to launderers of napkins and tablecloths, from cutlery and crockery suppliers to purveyors of soft drinks, water, wine, beers and spirits.

'To him, one brand of beer is just one of the hundreds of items he serves in his restaurant,' says Bilimoria. 'So you have got to make sure you are at the front of his mind, and that means being proactive. However much the restaurateur may love your product, with so much on his plate he may not be proactively ordering your products until, of course, it becomes a must-stock item. If his customers are clamouring for the product, he knows it is a priority and it becomes part of his routine, but in the early days it's not part of the routine. So you have got to follow up. You have got to do those regular telesales.'

Once a small company like Cobra, just starting out, is a given a chance, the product or service has to deliver. And the re-order rate is good test of whether the product works or not. In Cobra's case once the team had implemented a regular follow-up policy, the re-ordering rate went up to almost 100 per cent.

'It's simple really,' says Bilimoria. 'You should always put yourselves in the shoes of your customer and try to see things from their perspective.'

Using Bilimoria and Reddy's brand of hands-on sales strategy, the Cobra team very quickly built a base of around 100 restaurants Cobra supplied regularly. And it wasn't long before the company's rapid success attracted the attention of one of the distributors who had turned them down earlier in the year.

INTEGRATE YOUR MARKETING

With the sales and distribution side working well, Bilimoria turned his attention to marketing. Up to now the marketing budget had been minimal. The

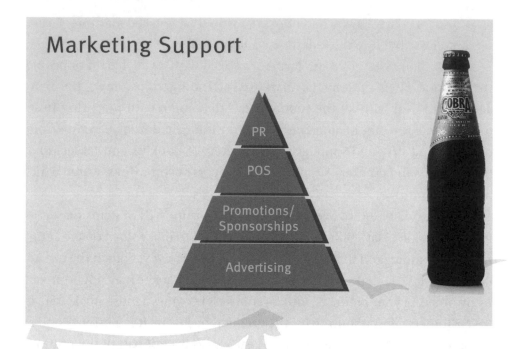

Marketing Support

first point of sale material, designed by the ad agency that Bilimoria's brother Nadir ran, was a flimsy cardboard table card in green and black print (because Bilimoria could not afford full colour) just giving an explanation of what Cobra beer was and where it was from.

Cobra was still not at the point where it could afford to recruit a heavy-weight ad agency, but there were ways of getting good PR other than throwing a lot of money at the problem (as Richard Branson, an entrepreneur much admired by Bilimoria, has demonstrated). Bilimoria wasn't about to fly around the world in a hot air balloon, though, or strip off his clothes brandishing a bottle of Cobra beer. Instead of putting himself in the photographer's frame, he let his beer take centre stage.

Free product, strategically dispensed, can often be a good way of attracting publicity and building a brand. It is a promotion tactic that Bilimoria has used very effectively. When he heard that Channel Four was launching a new series on the Indian food revolution in Britain, fronted by Ismail Merchant, the Indian film producer, Bilimoria contacted the programme makers and offered to provide the beer for the launch party at the Red Fort in Soho. The offer was accepted and Bilimoria invited along to the party.

Among the many people that Bilimoria met at the party was Iqbal Wahhab, a young journalist of Bangladeshi origin. Wahhab was a graduate of the London School of Economics, where he edited the university's student newspaper, *The Beaver*, and had become a prolific contributor to *The Independent*. The two men hit it off and agreed to meet for a drink shortly afterwards.

Wahhab told Bilimoria that he was getting out of journalism and setting up his own PR company, East-West Communications. He asked if Bilimoria would like to be his first client. The Cobra founder was already thinking about PR and had negotiated with a leading restaurant PR firm in London. However, Reddy had vetoed any appointment at that point, on the grounds that the quoted fee of £1500 a month was too expensive. Wahhab agreed to work for £1000 and Bilimoria persuaded Reddy that they should take him on.

It turned out to be a wise decision as the company began to work proactively on the PR side, getting media interviews, and building profile. 'We realised the power of public relations with a consumer brand, even when you are very, very small,' says Bilimoria. 'I learnt very early on that people are not going to write about you for the sake of it, but they will write about you if you are doing something genuinely interesting.'

Bilimoria reckons that everyone from the consumer to the brand manager tends to place too much emphasis on the role of advertising. 'I believe integrated marketing works best' he says. 'If you start with nothing, then you learn to make the most of everything. Richard Branson expresses this very well when he says that a big company will spend £10m on advertising a year, but will think ten times about spending £50,000 on public relations. Public relations does not always cost that much, but it can be hugely beneficial, especially with a consumer brand.'

Wahhab soon proved the value of hiring a PR firm. Shortly after he joined Cobra, the Wiltshire Brewery was put up for sale and offered to both Bilimoria and Bilimoria's rival Vijay Mallya, the owner of Indian company United Breweries, the Indian giant which makes Kingfisher beer. Wahhab contacted a journalist on *The Times* called Rajeev Syal, the brother of the writer and actress Meera Syal, and pitched a piece to him centred on the rivalry between Cobra and Kingfisher in Britain.

KARAN'S BUSINESS TIPS:
ON GOOD COMMUNICATION

Bilimoria is well aware of the importance of good communication. He will scribble notes to his staff, get on the phone, wherever he is in the world. He will conference himself into calls if he can't make a meeting. If he is in the country he will try to speak directly to each of the management team individually, and makes a point with the company meeting to address the team.

And then every Friday evening whoever is in the head office at 5.15–5.30 gathers around while Bilimoria, very informally, conveys news and updates, recaps major events, congratulates people, and does a round-up from the management team, getting people involved and making them feel a part of the company.

'Vijay Mallya had a huge giant of a business in India, started by his father decades earlier, whereas I had just started my business,' says Bilimoria. 'But the way the journalist wrote the article positioned Cobra as something of an equal of United.' The piece in *the Times* generated a lot of publicity for Cobra and helped raise awareness among the public. It was an instructive lesson in the power of the press.

COOKING UP *TANDOORI*

Cobra soon had a small sales team of four people in place, as well as the PR services of Wahhab. The company had tried various marketing tactics. Promotions have always been a popular Cobra tactic, from the 1992 free curry, free beer, promotion through to 'Win Free Cobra Beer for a Year', (a bottle a day) where the winners got sixteen cases of 330ml bottles as a prize, which actually works out at over 365 bottles. At the time, however, the team was still finding it difficult to reach out to the Indian restaurants. And they needed to, because most of the selling was direct to the restaurants and then fulfilled by the distributors.

There were very few chains of Indian restaurants. Even now the biggest chain of Indian restaurants is probably less than 20 restaurants strong. The restaurants tend to be individually owner managed, or in groups of two or three. So finding a way to get to the restaurants was very difficult for Cobra; the sales team wasn't big enough and the company couldn't afford the kind of advertising that was needed.

One obvious tactic was a mailshot, which Bilimoria tried. He does not have fond memories of the experience though. 'If you work out the cost, even if you do second class post, going out to over 6000 licensed restaurants, 6000 multiplied by 20p and the stationery and the envelopes and printing costs – its pretty expensive stuff,' says Bilimoria.

Trade advertising can be a cost effective way of advertising. Bilimoria thought the company's money would be better spent advertising in a trade magazine that went out regularly to all the Indian restaurants. There was only one problem. There wasn't one. So, as befits an entrepreneur, Bilimoria decided to start one.

The first call was to Pat Chapman, author of the *Good Curry Guide*. Bilimoria describes him as 'one of the people who has been instrumental in the growth of the Indian food industry in this country'. When Bilimoria contacted him, Chapman had just sold his membership organisation, the Curry Club of Great Britain but still had the rights to publish the *Good Curry Guide* and was looking for someone to sponsor the next edition. Cobra backed the 1992 issue and has sponsored it ever since. The next edition will be 2007

Chapman jumped at the chance to get involved in Bilimoria's magazine venture, and he brought with him his database of the names and addresses of every Indian restaurant in Britain. He got ten per cent of the shares of the new venture, with Bilimoria and Wahhab holding 45 per cent apiece. *Tandoori* magazine launched in September 1994. Bilimoria was the publisher and looked after the commercial side of the title, Wahhab edited it, and Chapman was a contributor. In reality everyone mucked in as required, with Bilimoria and his wife Heather helping proof-read the first few issues.

INTRODUCING DAVE

As the box shows, brand is an essential part of obtaining competitive advantage. From day one Bilimoria had an idea of what his beer brand should be like, what it represented and stood for. Those ideas crystallised through the

KEY ELEMENTS OF SUCCESSFUL BRANDING IN CREATING COMPETITIVE ADVANTAGE:

- **It aids consumer decision making and brand preferences:** A successful brand generates consumer trust which shortens their information processing time and enables preferences to be established and ingrained ahead of competitive offerings.

- **It helps build brand loyalty:** Brand preference generates repeat purchasing patterns that are difficult for the competition to emulate. Consistent repeat purchasing leads to greater sales and the likelihood of consumer advocacy and positive word of mouth.

- **Generates higher margins and improved shareholder value:** The no. 1 brand in a category will have more loyal customers than its nearest rivals and can usually charge a price premium; this is likely to lead to higher margins, reduced sales volatility and increases in shareholder value.

- **It can favourably influence other stakeholders beyond customers:** A strong brand reputation can facilitate access to markets through the equity created with distribution agents, improve employee retention and attract potential employees who are simply drawn by the brand name. Under the umbrella of a strong brand name and reputation, the risk of product development is reduced as existing consumer awareness and preference can facilitate more rapid trial.

Simon Knox, Professor of Brand Marketing,
Cranfield School of Management

formative years of the business. For most consumers, the idea of a brand is synonymous with advertising. And so it was that by the mid 1990s Bilimoria was ready to take Cobra's marketing to the next stage and embark on an advertising campaign.

By 1996 Bilimoria had bought his business partner, Reddy, out of the business. Sales had doubled in 1996 and new packaging had been introduced. It was time to appoint an ad agency. As it turned out it was a period of change for the company's marketing and PR.

After a beauty parade, during which Bilimoria met with a number of leading ad agencies, Team Saatchi was appointed. The company was introduced

Karan with his family in India, circa 1969.
From left to right: Karan, younger brother Nadir,
father Faridoon – then a Lieutenant Colonel in the Indian Army,
and later a Lieutenant General – and mother Yasmin.

Karan poses with his Cambridge University polo team in 1988.
It was at Cambridge that the inspiration for Cobra struck –
and indeed, Karan's start in business very appropriately came
when he began importing polo sticks from India
and selling them to Harrods and Lillywhites

Karan and Cobra co-founder Arjun Reddy
at the official Cobra press launch in 1991.

The first ever design of a Cobra bottle label,
focussing on the extra smooth taste
– an attribute still communicated on the bottle today.

Karan and Dr Subroto Cariapa – the head brewmaster at Mysore Breweries, where Cobra was first brewed – enjoying a drink in a London pub in 1992.

Mysore Brewery in Bangalore, India, where Cobra was first brewed, in a photo from 1990.

Karan poses with business partner Arjun Reddy, left,
and Mr K. P. Balasubramanium outside Gandhi Oriental Foods
– Cobra's first major distributor – in Bow, East London, in 1991.

General Bilimoria, Karan's father, visits the Languedoc region of France
in search of the latest addition to the General Bilimoria Wine range – 2001.

Members of the Cobra management team on a retreat at Veuve Clicquot,
in the champagne-maker's Hotel du Marc in Reims, France – 2006.
From left to right: Dynshaw Italia, Chief Operating Officer and Finance Director;
Karan; Chris Edgcumbe-Rendle, Business Development Director;
Jaimin Chandarana, Financial Controller; Simon Edwards, Marketing Director,
and Samson Sohail, Sales Director.

With Prime Minister Tony Blair at a UK Trade & Investment event in India
in September, 2005. The Prime Minister had just announced
the creation of the Indo British Partnership Network,
which Karan serves as founding chairman.

In 2006, Cobra won a company-record 12 Gold medals
at the prestigious Monde Selection, Brussels, World Selection of Quality Awards.
The medal tally was more than any other beer brand in the world
for the second year running.

Newly appointed as the Lord Bilimoria, of Chelsea,
Karan poses with his wife, Heather, on the day of his introduction
to the House of Lords – 24 July 2006.

to the agency by its brewers in the UK, Charles Wells. Team Saatchi did the advertising for Charles Wells' beers such as Bombardier, while parent company Saatchi & Saatchi handled Carlsberg.

Once Bilimoria had decided on Team Saatchi the next task was to select a creative team. The brief was simple: establish Cobra as the best beer to drink with Indian food. By now Cobra had overtaken rival brand Kingfisher in the bottled beer market, but was still behind Kingfisher and Carlsberg in terms of overall beer sales, draught, bottles and cans. So that placed Cobra as number three. Now Bilimoria wanted Cobra to be firmly established as the best beer to drink with Indian food. He also wanted the brand to make it onto the supermarket shelves.

All in all, five creative teams pitched for the account within Team Saatchi. The pitch that won Bilimoria over in the end was Curryholic Dave, and went something like this:

'We have got to have a spokesman for curryholics. So what we are going to do is use this term "curryholic" which is the fact that Britain is addicted to curry – emotionally and physically. So we are going to have a spokesman for curryholics and he is going give messages to fellow curryholics.' Brilliant.

Bilimoria was sold on the curryholic concept. But it still needed some work. Doing things differently is part of Bilimoria's genetic make up and runs right through the way Cobra is run. It was the same dealing with the ad agency. With many companies the client and creative team don't get to meet. The relationship is managed through the account director. But that's not the way Bilimoria does business. He formed a personal relationship with the creative team, building a strong rapport with them. It meant that he could ensure the Cobra brand was protected and that he didn't have unsuitable advertising foisted on him. Ultimately it probably saved both agency, and client, time and money.

Bilimoria recalls how Curryholic Dave took shape. 'I said, "Come on guys, what should this Curryholic Dave look like – is he bald, thin, fat, slim, Indian, English, how old, how young? Are we going to offend people, not offend people – appeal to some people, not appeal to some people? I am not sure about this spokesman idea of yours but I like the route. How can we get around this?"'

At which point the creative team came up with the idea of the person with the iconic brown takeaway bag over the head, two holes cut out for the eyes, and scribbled on the bag: "My name is Dave and I am a curryholic". Bilimoria had a long checklist for the Cobra ad. It had to be impactful, it had to make people turn round and look, it had to bring a smile to people's faces, it had to be quirky. Curryholic Dave ticked all the boxes. The tagline was 'The Beer from Bangalore, that let's you eat more – Curry'. (The tagline was subsequently changed after a run in with the Advertising Standards Agency. The follow up was 'The beer curryholics adore. It lets them eat more'.)

This was the first time that Cobra had spent significant sums on its advertising. The budget, still tiny for outfits like Team Saatchi, was an actual spend of £150,000 for the first three months. Total campaign costs, including agency costs, printing costs, materials, designs, etc. were £350,000 for a three month campaign, which was still not considered a lot of money for an ad campaign.

Bilimoria was determined to get the most impact for his money. The campaign ran on Capital Radio for three months, there were cross-track posters on the underground, a fly poster campaign, press coverage and postcards in cinemas. Cobra, it seemed, was everywhere. A survey of Londoners subsequently showed that 58 per cent of those polled had seen the ads and 96 per cent liked them.

But would it make any difference to the sales? Bilimoria need not have worried. The campaign got the company off to a flying start in January 1998. The supermarket listings began to happen. Draught installations increased. Sales maintained their upwards trajectory at a phenomenal 70 per cent growth rate having doubled the previous year. The three campaigns created by Team Saatchi between 1998 and 2000 were nominated for eight creative awards and won four.

MADE IN INDIA

As a company grows there may come a time when it needs to step up the marketing and consider television and radio advertising. That time eventually arrived with Cobra, and the company's experience of ramping up its advertising is a lesson to other companies that are looking to squeeze value out of the marketing budget.

By 2001, despite the success of the Curryholic Dave advertising, Bilimoria was keen to extend Cobra's reach to the mainstream. Cobra's victory at the Monde Selection World Quality Awards in 2001 in Brussels, where Cobra Beer won a gold medal, made Bilimoria even more determined to extend Cobra's customer base beyond the Indian restaurant sector, while at the same time increasing restaurant sales.

There was still plenty of scope for increasing sales to the Indian restaurants but it was important not to neglect the general beer drinker. Team Saatchi, however, was reluctant to abandon Curryholic Dave to his paper bag. Sensing a creative impasse Cobra switched to another leading advertising agency, McCann-Erickson.

McCann-Erickson's campaign was a bold campaign focused on the fact that Cobra was less gassy than other beers ('No Pressure') and that it was premium product – 'Three Cobras for the price of three'. Bilimoria describes it as 'very confident advertising'. Another tagline was: 'If you like Cobra, drink Cobra'. The campaign was built around the strap-line 'The less gassy bottled beer that puts you under no pressure'.

While Bilimoria liked the campaign, he found it difficult to take it any further working with McCann-Erickson. Eventually he relented and returned to Team Saatchi for Cobra's next change of advertising. The result was a campaign on the theme of Indian ingenuity. Saatchi chief executive Mike Parker later said: 'With the second campaign – Indian ingenuity – we were rightly asked to continue to build on the heritage of "Indian-ness". The focus has to remain on the Indian restaurateur and the ads have to be acceptable to him.' The new Saatchi campaign included the celebrated line: 'Ingenious because less gaseous'.

By 2002, an excited Bilimoria was ready to commission Cobra's first television and cinema commercials. The idea was for them to have an Indian flavour. Saatchi wanted to produce them in India, and Bilimoria said that was okay. He liked the ideas too. But he wasn't so keen on the price

'They came up with great ideas for these campaigns,' he says. 'Then they showed me the budget to produce the commercials. I nearly fell off my chair. It was $1m.' Bilimoria asked why it was so expensive. On top of the $1million, there was still the cost of paying for the airtime to show them on cinema and TV.

Saatchi explained. Apart from the production costs, there was the cost of taking the producer, the film director, the cast, the crew, and the equipment, to the shoot in India. And after shooting the ad, everyone and everything had to be brought back.

In reality, the ad agency suggested, it was a cost reduction, as a brand like Guinness or Stella might spend $1m producing one commercial, and the agency was producing two commercials. So it was two for the price of one.

But Bilimoria had an idea. Didn't Bollywood, the Indian based film-industry centred on Mumbai, produce more films than Hollywood each year? Had Saatchi considered that India has a highly developed commercial advertising industry? The agency responded that the quality wouldn't be good enough. That was red rag to a bull.

By this point Cobra had just set up an office in India. Bilimoria made some enquiries, short-listed the top commercial production companies in India, before selecting one of the leading companies, and one of the leading directors. Then Bilimoria persuaded the people at Saatchi to use Indian resources. In the end, because the Saatchi team used an Indian crew, an Indian cast, shot and edited the ad on location in India, only two people flew out from Team Saatchi in the UK. The commercials were produced at a fraction of Saatchi's original $1m budget – a win for Britain and British creativity, a win for India and Indian resources, and a win for Cobra Beer.

According to Bilimoria, the people at Saatchi were 'gobsmacked' by the quality of the finished result and subsequently used the same director on other projects.

The commercials – one, 'Carwash', featured a car washing service that used elephants to spray its customers' vehicles – were screened on Channel 4, E4, Virgin Atlantic flights, the Cobra website, as well as running as a national cinema campaign. As a result of Bilimoria breaking the usual ad filming conventions, there was some spill-over publicity too. The story of how the advertising was produced later featured as a case study on an edition of *Newsnight* that looked at the potential for creative links between Britain and India.

The new campaign had the desired effect on sales. However, Cobra's increased visibility, as it joined the charmed circle of lager brands that advertised on television and broke into the Top 20 beer brands in the UK, also had one entirely unexpected consequence.

'These adverts were shown in 2003, and towards the end of 2003 we got a phone call from Mike Parker at Saatchi & Saatchi Group who asked to see me that same day,' says Bilimoria. 'I said fine. Everything was going well. We were more than happy with the commercials. Indeed, we were thinking of how we were going to take things forward.'

When Parker arrived at Cobra's HQ and sat down in Bilimoria's office he had some unexpected news. Team Saatchi had to resign the Cobra account. Bilimoria was astonished, until he heard why. As Parker explained the situation it transpired that Cobra was a victim of its own success.

Carlsberg, one of Cobra's competitors, was a long standing client of Saatchi & Saatchi, the main agency. When Cobra first signed up with Team Saatchi back in 1997 this wasn't a problem, presumably because Cobra didn't really appear on the 'competitors of Carlsberg' radar. But now, in part due to the success of the advertising work by Team Saatchi, the client conflict was significant enough to lead the point where Parker was sitting in Bilimoria's office breaking the bad news.

It would not have been in character for Bilimoria to accept the news without a fight. Sure enough Bilimoria resolved to challenge the decision, taking Cobra's case as high as Saatchis' head of Europe. But, in the end, there was nothing for it but to announce the split, which was done with a press release entitled: 'Team Saatchi Resigns Cobra'.

The body copy read: 'Team Saatchi has resigned the Cobra account. The decision recognises the potential for conflict of interest with Carlsberg-Tetley, a long-standing client in the Saatchi & Saatchi Group, as the two companies are increasingly competitive in the Indian restaurant sector.' It added: 'We are enormously proud of the work we have created for Cobra and are sorry that the relationship has come to an end.'

Even today, some years after, the experience rankles with Bilimoria. From a simple commercial perspective, Bilimoria finds the mores of the advertising business in relation to client conflict slightly baffling. 'If an advertising agency has one beer brand, they feel they cannot take on another beer brand,' he says. 'I find that very strange. In the accountancy industry, for example, Ernst & Young as a firm will have a lot of breweries as clients because they are seen as experts in the brewing industry. It is not a problem with any of the breweries. They know they are dealing with a professional firm, with professional standards including that of client confidentiality. If anything, it is a benefit that Ernst & Young knows the so industry well. I wouldn't mind if my advertising agency had three or four other beer brands. In fact, I would quite like that.'

As it stood there was nothing for it but to put the advertising account out to pitch once more. This time the beauty parade was a little different. By now Cobra Beer was a trophy client, and the best agencies in town were queuing up to win its business. The account was eventually awarded to a boutique agency called Joshua, part of Grey Worldwide. Joshua had just been named 'Advertising Agency of the Year' in Britain for its creative work.

The move, though enforced and unexpected, proved to be a fortuitous one as the new injection of creativity and a fresh perspective did wonders for the brands' marketing. It is a lesson for other businesses: when it comes to advertising, a change is frequently as good as a rest. Bilimoria would not have moved the account for a while had he not been forced to. 'With hindsight it was a fabulous move,' says Bilimoria. 'The new agency has done some phenomenal work for us.'

Straplines have included: 'An inspired blend of hops, maize, yeast, barley, malt, rice and *determination*', and another using the same words ending with '... *imagination*'. The new campaigns have run on Tube posters and in men's magazines.

EXTENDING THE BRAND

For years, the company stuck with its core range of 660ml and 330ml bottles and 50 litre kegs, containing a beer that was five per cent alcohol by volume. But, with the launch of Browar Belgia's canned Cobra, Bilimoria decided it was time to take the bold, and risky, step of extending the brand.

The first brand extension was a non-alcoholic version. 'Every single non-alcoholic beer we had ever tasted was awful,' says Bilimoria. 'Why couldn't we produce a good non-alcoholic beer?' It was a perfect example of a market

COBRAVISON

CobraVison is the inspired invention of Cobra's new creative agency Joshua, who in collaboration with Bilimoria, came up with a groundbreaking initiative that allow budding filmmakers the opportunity to showcase their short films on ITV2, ITV3 and ITV4.

Cobra's £1m sponsorship of the movies on the ITV channels allows it to run the competition winning film-shorts as five-second extracts in eight to ten slots per movie, seven days a week. The 2005 slots, which were seen by an average of 500,000 people each time, ran with the strap line 'Inspired'. The contract with ITV was renewed and extended to ITV4 in 2006 and the branding slots increased to 10 seconds.

The winning filmmakers are celebrated at an awards ceremony in April, where the best of the best win some fantastic prizes including a trip to India, cash prizes ... and lots of Cobra Beer.

CobraVision took bumper advertisements and did them in a way never done before anywhere in the world – another example of being different, better, and changing the marketplace forever.

in which Cobra could do something differently, better and change the marketplace forever.

Bilimoria could see three obvious markets for a non-alcoholic version of Cobra: teetotallers – individuals who don't drink at all either for religious reasons or through personal choice; car users who don't want to drink and drive; and people who don't like drinking at lunchtime.

The key would be to develop a product that remained true to the Cobra taste. The two most common ways of making non-alcoholic beer are to brew it but not ferment it, so it resembles a malt beverage, or to brew it and ferment it as a beer, and then extract the alcohol but that can create – in Bilimoria's words – 'a very harsh, sharp, artificial sort of taste'.

Bilimoria's team tracked down an independent brewery in Holland, called Bavaria Breweries, which uses proprietary technology and ingredients that enable it to brew non-alcoholic beer in the same way as a normal beer. It both brews and ferments during the production process using a special yeast that doesn't create alcohol. It then goes to Poland, where Cobra's own hops are added.

Cobra 0.0% was launched in January 2005, and the critics liked it. One taste test in *the Daily Mirror* gave it 9/10 and described it as 'Head and shoulders above the rest'.

Emboldened by the success of Cobra 0.0%, Bilimoria shifted his attention to the low calorie market. Light beers have taken the US, in particular, by storm. Bud Lite, for example, is a bigger brand than Budweiser and light beers are particularly popular with women. But Bilimoria found many of them bland and insipid. There was a gap in the market for a lower calorie and lower carbohydrate beer that lived up to the quality of the Cobra band.

Six months after Cobra 0.0% was launched Cobra brought out Cobra Lower Cal. It is still a premium lager with an ABV 4.3 per cent. It just has fewer calories: under 100 calories in a 330ml bottle, a reduction of more than 25 per cent on the original brand. Indeed, with 95 calories and 4.1g of carbohydrate, Cobra Lower Cal is lighter than many of its competitors, including Michelob Ultra (106 calories, 3g), Coors Light (102, 5) and Bud Light (110, 6.6).

KARAN SAYS:

- Hire for will, not skill.
- My father's advice to me: it's important to have not just an efficient team but a *happy* and efficient team.
- There two kinds of leaders, leaders who are charismatic and leaders who are inspirational. One rarely comes across leaders who are both charismatic and inspirational. Two examples are Nelson Mandela and Mahatma Gandhi.
- Give people respect and give people trust.
- It's important to not just do things right, but to do the right thing.
- Don't just try to be the best in the world, be the best *for* the world.
- The difference between education, knowledge, and business:
  1) Education is learning
  2) Knowledge is understanding
  3) Business is application
- Knowledge; Application. Ideas; Action. Aspire; Achieve.

CHAPTER SEVEN

RESTLESS INNOVATION

nnovation has always been the key to creating a successful business. The
difference today is that advances in technology and communications
mean that competitive advantage through innovation is often fleeting.

Bilimoria is well aware of the need for Cobra to stay one step ahead of the
competition. That is why he is a firm believer not only in innovation, but in
restless innovation. The innovative spirit is captured in the company's guid-
ing principle: 'Different, better, changing the marketplace forever'.

THE COBRA GLASS

When the first bottles of Cobra were distributed to restaurants, the only
point-of-sale material on offer to restaurants was a flimsy table card made
from cardboard and designed by an ad agency headed by Bilimoria's brother,
Nadir. It was printed in black and green, because the company could not
afford a full colour version.

As soon as it was financially viable, however, Bilimoria focused attention
on improving the point-of-sale offering. His customers, the Indian restaurants, were clamouring for branded beer glasses, so Bilimoria decided to
supply some.

Determined that the Cobra beer glass would outshine anything else in the
restaurants, he arranged a meeting with a sales team from German manufacturer SAHM, widely considered to be the best beer glass makers in the world.
After reviewing the company's catalogue, however, Bilimoria noticed that
almost all the glasses on show had either a badge or crest to show which com-

pany, or brand they were associated with. The only real difference between them was the shape of the glass. The question was: what could they do to ensure that Cobra's glasses stood out from all the others?

Bilimoria and his team set to work on the problem. One suggestion was that the glass should be fluted, and eventually they also settled on a gold rim. On the body of the glass the idea was to have a large map of India, with Bangalore highlighted, to stress Cobra's heritage.

The glasses were a great success, so much so that they became an instant collector's item. Customer's started taking them away from restaurants; some would ask, some simply stuffed one into a bag when the waiter's back was turned. The new glasses didn't just make an impact with collectors though, they made an impact on the company's sales. 'We brought in those beer glasses and our sales in the Indian restaurants went up by 50 per cent in six months,' says Bilimoria. 'Just because of those glasses. They were an instant hit.'

KARAN'S BUSINESS TIPS: CREATIVE FRICTION

Because of the atmosphere at Cobra it encourages people to come up with ideas, to make things happen, sometimes that will cause friction. Bilimoria believes that, in an open enough atmosphere, this friction is almost a positive thing.

'The important thing there is that once you have made the decision as a team, you are bound to it,' he says ' You can have the arguments, you can have the debates, you can say, I don't agree with this, or it should be … or a different manager wants to do things this way. And I think having that healthy debate is actually a very good thing. But once you have made a team decision, then everyone should bind to it and run with it.'

MAKING INNOVATION HAPPEN

Saying that an organisation should have a culture of restless innovation is one thing, but how do you make it happen? How can you get that into your business? What structures do you need? What kind of practical things can you do that will make it easier to innovate, and to get ideas into action?

First you need to be aware of how important innovation is, Bilimoria says. You must recognise that being innovative is one of the key factors to success, to growing a brand, and growing a business. Second is the state of mind – it is an attitude. You must have the confidence to innovate and to encourage everyone around you to constantly innovate.

Then you have to make that innovation happen. That links into creating an environment in your business where you are constantly encouraging people to come up with ideas, and constantly encouraging people to enable those ideas and make them happen.

At Cobra Beer it means keeping an open atmosphere in your office where you literally have very few rules, where you encourage people from all parts of the company to come up with ideas.

You can have mechanisms that encourage this. So in Cobra's case, for example, it has the 'idea of the month'. An empty box of Cobra serves as an ideas box, and everyone from the company is encouraged to put in ideas over the course of the month. One volunteer from the company goes through the ideas and selects the best three ideas of the month and they are recognised, acknowledged, and rewarded at the monthly company meeting. Most importantly, they are put into action.

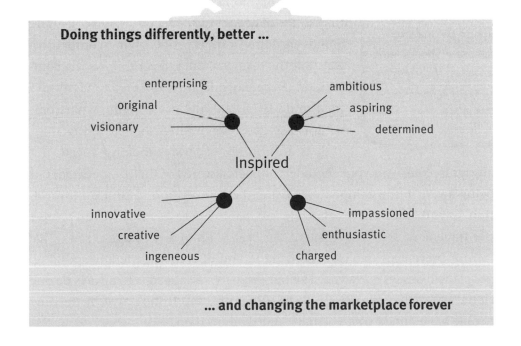

Doing things differently, better ...

enterprising
original
visionary

ambitious
aspiring
determined

Inspired

innovative
creative
ingeneous

impassioned
enthusiastic
charged

... and changing the marketplace forever

HIDEAWAYS AND SWOT ANALYSIS

Once or twice a year, Cobra's senior management leave behind the ringing phones and queues of supplicants that bedevil the life of every manager trying to do a spot of blue-sky thinking and meet somewhere outside the office to ponder the future. These gatherings are known as 'hideaways'.

A potent planning weapon, hideaways have produced defining moments in the Cobra story. Important tools at hideaways: flipcharts, fresh notepads, an open mind. Activities: strategising and brainstorming. An essential feature of the hideaway is performing a SWOT analysis: a survey of the company's Strengths, Weaknesses, Opportunities, and – above all – Threats.

These ideas might be marketing ideas that have been put forward from somebody in the accounts department, or it could be an idea to do with draught beer that was suggested by somebody in marketing – something you would have expected a sales person to come up with. Then there is a follow-up scheme where somebody makes sure that the ideas are implemented.

An important part of this process is not just the aspect of generating ideas, but that the process makes everyone in the company feel a part of the overall business – the overall brand – and not just part of their particular speciality. It promotes integration and cross silo working, it breaks down barriers. It is a virtuous circle, because the more open the environment, the more innovation there is.

Another part of making innovation happen, says Bilimoria, is to pay attention to what the competition is doing, while making sure that you don't copy or imitate. Bilimoria always encourages his people to be aware of what other beer brands and consumer brands are doing. It spurs people on in a competitive way. But the team at Cobra never follows the competition. From day one, the Cobra team has always tried to do its own thing, not copying what competitors like Carlsberg or Kingfisher are doing.

'It is an attitude of always looking ahead, not always looking over your shoulder; not being scared of the competition, but being aware of the competition. Using the competition to spur on innovation,' says Bilimoria. 'We acknowledge that, in our case, while we can protect our trademark, we cannot patent our beer – not in any practical sense. We cannot prevent people from copying it, and of course, generally speaking, people will always copy you. The only way to stay ahead is to always be one step ahead of the competition. So by being constantly innovative, by the time people have copied you, you have already moved on.'

MAKING THE IMPOSSIBLE POSSIBLE?

Bilimoria's concern with 'restless innovation' extends to all of the aspects of the business, as it should in all businesses. That includes the smallest details; like the bottles the beer comes in. It also means open innovation, sharing the innovation process with expert advisors whenever relevant.

In April 2002, Bilimoria was visiting his family in Dehradun, India, in the foothills of the Himalayas, when he suddenly decided Cobra's packaging needed to be updated. The packaging had remained unchanged for the previous five years, ever since the company started brewing at Charles Wells.

With sales going well there was some internal resistance at what was viewed as unnecessary expenditure. When Bilimoria called to discuss the redesign, Simon Edwards, Cobra's marketing director, attempted to persuade Bilimoria that the existing format was fine, but Bilimoria was adamant and so a number of design agencies were invited to pitch for the work.

Three of the UK's top design agencies pitched for the account, with award-winning agency Williams Murray Hamm securing the business. Bilimoria was impressed with the agency's desire to move things forward rather than just tinker with the existing design. 'I was really encouraged by the agency's attitude when we visited for the final pitch,' says Bilimoria. 'Richard Murray, one of the partners, promised it would not be a question of rearranging the furniture.'

Murray explained what he meant using two examples. Turning to what he called his 'naughty cupboard' he pulled out two bottles of whisky. After asking the Cobra team to spot the difference between them – which they did with some difficulty – he asked them to nominate which one was the redesigned version. No one could make up their mind. He then did the same with two brands of cooking sauces, with an identical result.

'We call this rearranging the furniture,' he said. 'We will never just change for the sake of changing. If we change, you will notice it and there will be a reason for it. And it is not just going to look pretty.' Bilimoria's mind was made up: 'These are the guys for us, I thought.'

Williams Murray Hamm embarked on its own research into the brand. The initial findings were much as expected: people liked Cobra beer because of its extra smooth and less gassy taste. As Bilimoria said: 'We could have told you that!'

After wrestling with a way of communicating the consumer feedback via the label, the agency decided to go back to the drawing board. It was then that inspiration struck. The smoothness wasn't all that customers commented on. Another thing that people commented on was how Cobra had become virtually a household name in a comparatively short space of time – just 12 years. This led the agency to think of ways of portraying the history behind the company on the packaging.

The agency drew on the example of architectural columns from ancient civilizations such as the Romans, Persians, Greeks, Egyptians and Indians which tell stories through reliefs, sculptures and hieroglyphs. It proposed telling the story of Cobra Beer through a series of icons embossed on the bottle.

Bilimoria was keen on the idea but, as is often the case with new innovations, there were many obstacles to overcome before the idea became a reality. For example, according to Bilimoria, the first reaction from the people at Cobra's bottle manufacturer Rockware Glass was 'forget it'. They protested that the embossing was so intricate that it would present all sorts of quality control issues, quite apart from design problems and strength problems.

'Of course we listened,' Bilimoria says. 'We worked with Rockware and modified the design, but in the end we made possible something that was perceived as impossible. Rockware Glass is justly proud of the end result and it has won award after award for packaging design.'

The new bottle was launched with a great fanfare at a party in a London wine cellar on 28 July 2003. Cobra staff mingled with customers, investors, suppliers, journalists, City bankers, lawyers and suppliers. There was even a television crew in attendance. The entire exercise, including concept and design fees and the cost of new moulds, had cost £110,000 but Bilimoria thought it well worth the money.

Today, each bottle is embossed with six Cobra icons: a family crest (denoting the general's son) a mother elephant and her calf (learning lessons in lager), a snake charmer (charming beer), a pair of scales (against all odds), two palm trees next to a building (from Bangalore to Bedford), and a boat carrying beer barrels (around the world).

'It's the first time in the world that a product tells its story visually as part of its packaging,' says Bilimoria proudly.

1. THE GENERAL'S SON

2. LEARNING LESSONS IN LAGER

3. CHARMING BEER

4. AGAINST ALL ODDS

5. FROM BANGALORE TO BEDFORD

6. AROUND THE WORLD

KING COBRA

Product innovation is key for a company that survives on the strength of its product offering. However, product innovation can be a double-edged sword. Tinkering with a well-known brand can be a risky strategy, so if a company decides to do that, they need to make sure that they get it right. It shouldn't be innovation for the sake of it.

When Robert Goizueta made the 'the boldest single marketing move in the history of the consumer goods business' replacing classic Coca-Cola with New Coke it proved to be a case study marketing blunder. The very idea of 'New Coke' was an antithesis to the brand values of tradition and authenticity. Normally die-hard loyal Coke fans claimed the new formula tasted 'too sweet' and 'flat'. It wasn't long before Classic Coke was back.

In 2005 Cobra decided to bring an innovative new product to market. The extra strong lager market had a bit of an image problem. Bilimoria wanted to change this perception by creating an upmarket strong lager, and with the help of his management team began playing with ideas for a drink which would have more in common with beers rooted in the Belgian Trappist tradition: high quality, flavoursome lagers that were often eight per cent alcohol.

KARAN'S BUSINESS TIPS:
FASHIONING A EUREKA MOMENT

Genius may well be one per cent inspiration, ninety-nine per cent perspiration, as Thomas Alva Edison, the great US inventor claimed. That one per cent is pretty important though, and probably the most elusive element of genius.

Ideas and innovation, as we have seen throughout this book, are the currency in which entrepreneurs trade. Yet ideas are not always that easy to come by. Pythagoras, the Greek mathematician and philosopher had one of his greatest ideas in the bath. But is there anything that we can do to help bring on our own eureka moment?

Bilimoria recalls a lecture he attended where a Cambridge professor was talking about the 'eureka moment'. The professor, who had studied the idea of the eureka moment in some depth, related how Pythagoras had, prior to his revelatory bath, been in the classroom focusing intently on the mathematical solution to a problem.

It was only when he detached himself from the problem completely, switched off and lay in the bath relaxing, that the solution came to him suddenly. If he had continued persevering in the classroom, that moment of creative spark would not have happened.

'There is that element, that aspect of creativity where you need to have this intensive approach and then, alongside that, almost switch off,' says Bilimoria. 'Then it all suddenly falls into place. I find that a lot. Some of my best ideas come through when I am shaving or in the shower in the morning, or while I am on an aircraft. So, to be creative, I think you always need that balance in life – periods of intense activity, but also times when you are detached from work.'

There are seven Trappist breweries in the world, where traditional beer is brewed by the Trappist monks. Six are in Belgium: Achel, Chimay, Orval, Rochefort, Westmalle, and Westvleteren. La Trappe is in the Netherlands. In all, they produce about 20 fairly strong bottle-conditioned beers.

The vision was of a lager beer that would be a premium product, treated more like wine than a pint of lager. Wine is normally 12–13 per cent alcohol and these types of Belgian beers are consumed almost like wine. They are savoured. It was a bold decision by Bilimoria.

Bilimoria and his management team mulled over numerous ideas for the new product, always mindful of the stigma against strong beer – to come up with something without the negative associations was a challenge.

But it was Koen Cruycke at Browar Belgia who suggested something truly original – a double-fermented, bottle-conditioned strong lager, the likes of which had never been seen before. And, with some justification, it would be called King Cobra.

In fact the brewing process is more akin to champagne production than lager beer. The beer is produced in Poland at eight per cent strength, at which point it has very little carbonation. It is then chilled in tankers to about four degrees, after which it is transported to the Rodenbach brewery in Belgium. This is one of the most famous brewers of traditional Belgian red ale in Belgium.

Once at Rodenbach a little bit of sugar is added, together with some Trappist ale lambic yeast, into the large champagne type bottles that are used. The bottles are corked and stored in cellars, where the temperature is raised to 25 degrees centigrade and secondary fermentation takes place in the bottles.

It is during this process that the yeast eradicates the sugar and carbonates the liquid in much the same way that the fizz is put into champagne. In the production of champagne, however, the bottles are tilted upside down and the yeast is allowed to settle in the top, where it is frozen and then removed.

With King Cobra, the yeast remains in the bottle where it settles at the bottom as a sediment. The secondary fermentation process completed, it is allowed to cool down for two weeks and then the beer is ready to drink.

'What you then have is an unpasteurised beer,' explains Bilimoria, 'which has a much longer shelf life than a pasteurised beer. If any oxygen gets into the bottle, the yeast gobbles it up. King Cobra has wonderful aroma, texture, smoothness and softness. It is a strong eight per cent lager. The "champagne" of beers.'

One of the main drivers behind the development of the new premium product was the Indian market, where more than 70 per cent of the beer sold is strong lager. And it would be a truly international beer – from an Anglo-Indian beer brand, developed by a Belgian brewmaster at a Polish brewery, and brewed in Poland and Belgium.

King Cobra was soon being stocked by all the main supermarket chains, including Tesco, Sainsbury's and Waitrose, as well as Selfridges; and Bilimoria is planning a series of packaging innovations, including miniature champagne bottles for bars and a canned version for the off trade. Meanwhile the Indian market will be given a more straightforward version, which has not been double-fermented.

THE HOFFMAN GROUP

When a bridge engineer called Ralph A. Hoffman proposed building a bridge across the Grand Canyon in Arizona at the beginning of the last century, he was ridiculed as a dreamer. But by 1929 his vision had been realised and the 833-foot-long Lees Ferry Bridge opened to traffic. Today, named the Navajo Bridge, it stands as a monument to the potency of thinking the unthinkable.

Hoffman's example so inspired the people at Cobra that they founded a brainstorming group in his honour and it meets regularly – every two months – to generate ideas on how to take the company forward. Meetings are normally preceded by a field visit, perhaps to a supermarket, and then – under the chairmanship of the marketing director Simon Edwards – members of the group put forward their ideas. The success of each gathering is measured in IPH (ideas per hour) and the record so far is 96.

Reading the minutes of the Hoffman Group meeting held on Wednesday 16 November 2005, it is soon apparent why Cobra is the success story that it is.

MINUTES OF HOFFMAN GROUP MEETING, WEDNESDAY 16 NOVEMBER 2005

TOPIC OF DISCUSSION: Touch points – Examples of touch points are the phone, internet, office, sales people, letters, invoices, etc); in short a touch point is anything that puts our customers in contact with Cobra.

The purpose of the Hoffman Group was to look at finding innovative ways of improving these points. First, the Hoffman Group discussed existing touch points. These were divided into broad categories. Next, its members offered ideas on how to improve some of our current touch points, and also suggested new touch points for the company.

We were encouraged to think of ways in which Cobra Beer interacts with its customers. Listed below are Cobra Beer's major touch points that the Hoffman Group came up with:

1 Events: Cobra's brand visibility is very important at events. Events that Cobra Beer sponsors are a reflection of the company and affect public perception of the brand.
2 Outlets selling Cobra: While technically divorced from the company (we have no direct connection with them), their behaviour affects the end consumer.
3 Website: A key touch point. Wholly controlled by and representative of Cobra Beer. A virtual image of the company, it can be a very powerful and useful tool.
4 Telephone: The opinions of customers and clients calling the company are directly influenced by the telephone manner of the employee who answers the phone.
5 On hold: The on-hold music, heard by anyone calling the company, is very important.
6 People coming in for meetings: They are touch points as we interact with them. They leave with opinions about the company and its atmosphere; they come in direct contact with Cobra Beer Ltd., which affects their judgement on Cobra Beer's products.
7 Emails: The way employees write emails, their signatures, attached logos, etc.
8 Answering machines: Messages left by employees reflect on the entire company's professionalism.
9 Cobra employees: Their interaction with customers and clients.

10   More information about colleague's jobs: Everyone should be more informed about more than just their job roles and their departments.

11   Goody bags: An impactful and very popular touch point

12   Third parties: Suppliers (especially POS), couriers, auditors, bankers etc.

13   Drivers and vans: Cobra's most visual touch points in the London area?

14   Office: The atmosphere, the buzz, the general tidiness of the office.

15   PR/advertising: Controls Cobra's image to the trade. Our advertising choices also demonstrate our character.

16   POS: Point of sale choices are carefully made, keeping in mind the image we want to project to the end consumer. Cobra's POS is not just a product in itself but an extension of our brand.

17   Sponsorships/events: The events we sponsor, the visibility of our product at the actual event and, if present, our employees, are all touch points

18   Sending out via DHL: Beer that is repackaged and sent out from our office

19   Consumers: All the people outside of Cobra Beer who come in touch with the brand and the company are consumers. Each one is a touch point.

20   Leaflets: Vital touch points used to educate and inform customers.

21   Letters/faxes/stationery: Office stationery; the choice of paper, colours, the fax cover sheet are aimed at customers and clients.

22   Karan: is a propeller of Cobra Beer and an enormously important touch point.

23   Directors: A powerful touch point projecting the power corridors (if those exist) of Cobra Beer.

24   GB Wines: Our wine range.

25   Charities and sponsorships: Sponsored charities reflect the causes we support. Cobra's link to select causes is a vital touch point in this field.

26   Word of mouth: Employees who talk to their friends about their work place; customers who recommend Cobra; anyone who mentions Cobra acts as a touch point to the people they talk to.

27   Menus: Wine menus we provide; restaurant menus in which Cobra is listed.

28   Awards and accolades: The press and news generated around the awards that Cobra and Karan receive is a great touch point, usually positive.

29 Sampling and tastings: Held by brand development executives or bar owners and a focal touch point; focusing on Cobra Beer they are a moment in time where there is interaction with potential new customers.

30 Trade shows: Touch points of intent, planned with deliberation; Cobra Beer wants to attract people to its stand.

31 Telesales: Talking to customers over the phone; the phone interaction is crucial to customers: telesales *are* Cobra Beer.

32 Business cards: The layout, the colours, our medals, what they say, all these factors influence people who receive them.

33 Cobra Minis: The branded cars are offered to Cobra employees and are a great way of advertising our brand.

34 CobraVision: An enormous touch point affecting so many aspects outside of Cobra Beer; ITV, the film makers, the production side of ITV, the viewers, the visitors to the website, CobraVision winners, etc.

35 Brewery/Wincanton: People interested in Cobra Beer will always view the breweries as an extension of the brand. Wincanton is responsible for the dispatch of our beer within the United Kingdom and consequently affects our major suppliers.

36 International offices: Mentioning Cobra Beer's international offices to people we talk to is a touch point, as is the perception of employees at the international offices of the headquarters.

37 Film community and other communities: The festivals we support, the communities we work with, CobraVision's interaction and presence at festivals and film-related events are all enormous touch points.

38 *Tandoori* magazine: A touch point for Cobra Beer through its advertising in the magazine, Cobra News and its presence in the Indian restaurant sector.

39 Journalists: Who interview Karan or the management team, speak to the PR team, and are powerful touch points.

40 Displays: Are a strong, eye-catching touch point.

41 Rewards of customer loyalty: The support that our company lends to its customers reflects the relationship that we share with them.

42 Brand partners: Cobra Beer chooses brand partners that fit in with the company's vision or mission

43 Route to market/distributors/C&C: These are Cobra Beer's major touch points and, in turn, they become touch points to the end consumer.

44 Cobra parties: At the summer party and Christmas party, Cobra Beer employees are clients and this is an interesting role reversal – we end up being served by our suppliers and are, no doubt, scrutinised and observed.

45 Complaints: The manner in which they are dealt with, the interaction between the office and the person or persons making a complaint is a crucial touch point which can have consequences that last beyond the mere complaint itself.

46 References/suppliers: Suppliers lead to contacts and references which could turn out to be new agents who are able to supply different things.

47 Supplier relationship: Any supplier automatically becomes a touch point; they have links with Cobra Beer and contribute to Cobra's overall image.

48 Interns: Interns who spend time at Cobra Beer are a significant touch point. Their experience as a Cobra employee may be brief but it helps them to form impressions of Cobra Beer with added insider's knowledge.

49 Shareholders/stakeholders: Shareholders' investment in Cobra Beer is a delicate relationship which, needless to say, needs to be handled with diplomacy and care.

50 Accounts: This refers more precisely to accounts payable when, for example, clients chase payment.

51 Internal department interaction: Although internal, this is an important touch point because the extent of our interaction with other departments is an indication of our perceptions of our colleagues.

SELECTED TOUCH POINTS AND SUGGESTIONS FOR IMPROVEMENT

OFFICE

1 Front door: The front door must be answered. The receptionist must not just open it for people who ring/buzz.

2 A sign for the front door that clearly displays Cobra Beer on it will help visitors identify it more easily.

3 Window sign: The office should have a window sign so that people passing in the street can see where Cobra Beer is.

4 Post room: The company needs a proper post room that accommodates the franking machine, bags and all the accoutrements of posting.

5   Uniform desk layout: The office needs a uniform desk layout so that everyone has just as much desk and leg room as the next person.

6   Re-designing the office: Following from the above point, the office is in need of a redesign.

7   Clear reception area: We received feedback that not having a clearly demarcated reception area confused people, especially when receptionists were not at their desks. Outsiders find themselves looking around helplessly for the first friendly face – not very professional.

8   Bar area for meetings: We need a bar area for meetings so that they are relaxed, quirky and cool – just like Cobra.

9   Plasma screen running Cobra Vision with sound.

10 Display area with POS: The office needs a display area to showcase inspirational POS ideas that Cobra employees pick up.

11 Quiet room: A place to retire to meditate, contemplate, resuscitate oneself (with some shut-eye perhaps) when the office is just too crazy to handle.

12 Play room with punch bag, PS2s, fooze ball – a place to retire to when the craziness of the office is too much to handle and where one's frustration can be discreetly unleashed.

13 The Inspired Room.

14 Themed afternoons based on inspired products.

15 Inspired corner to post things: Similar to the POS idea, a corner in the office where anything that inspires us can be put up for everyone else to see.

16 In-office massages.

17 Clean up days: Routine clean-up days, maybe for each department, so that Jobina (the office manager at the time) doesn't have to yell at us.

18 Tea person: A four o'clock 'tea person' who gives us our mid-afternoon pick-me-up cuppas.

19 Meetings outside: As much as possible.

20 Cobra Bar outdoors: Especially during summer, a portable bar for us to use/hire out for events.

PHONES

1   Personalised voicemail: All employees should have personalised voicemail so that people who contact us will know that they are dealing with the right person and aren't befuddled.

2 Scripts to help: Standard scripts for everyone who answers the phone to familiarise us with answering procedures. This should be included in every new office-based employee's kit.

3 Training for phone manager: Everyone needs to have phone manager training because you never know when you'll have to use it.

4 Standardised ways to answer phones: Phones are a basic and essential touch point. They may also be the most widely used touch point; everyone at Cobra should answer phones in a standard, polite and friendly manner.

5 General product fact sheet: So that everyone knows the basic information about our products.

6 Full time receptionists: Not office manager – as we did over the Christmas break.

7 Re-learn phone manager: With regular brush-up lessons.

8 Holding music: Should be rotated regularly; callers can now be pleasantly surprised and may actually not mind holding for someone.

9 Faxes via computer: To save on paper and fax confirmation sheets that just get thrown into the bin.

10 Downsize new signature: Because it's too big an attachment.

11 Personalised emails based on employee likes and dislikes: Our emails should change every day/week/month with a different signature.

12 Intranet photos: So that new employees can quickly get to know the rest of us, and we don't waste paper and time updating the organisational chart.

13 Organisational chart in corridors.

EVENTS

1 Complete event kit: A basic event kit that contains all the event requisites so that we don't have to scramble for things before an event.

2 Event fridges: To be kept here at the office to use for events.

3 Feedback/competition form: To get tips from fresh eyes outside the company.

4 Range of banners.

5 Event team/promo staff: A standard event team who knows how to organise an event; it will make things quick, efficient and easy.

6 Theatre behind the bar.

7 Thorough staff briefing before an event: Compulsory – no more throwing people in the deep end.

8   CobraVision explanation: Event staff need to be briefed on CobraVision.

9   Info blurb in between films: On TV.

10   Cobra plastic glasses: Branded – to use at events.

11   Branded tuk tuks (an auto-rickshaw).

EMPLOYEES

1   Cobra uniforms for drivers: They are our most visual touch point in London.

2   Website address on T-shirts: So that Cobra fans can satiate their curiosity.

3   Umbrellas: All types – golf, flapped, employees – for everyone to use. This is essential; London must be *the* rainiest city in the world!

4   New employee welcome kit: Which includes all the essentials discussed above, which is friendly and happy and has a come-play-with-me-and-find-out-everything-about-Cobra quality to it.

5   Branded business card cases: So that we don't waste hundreds of cards because they become smudgy and crumpled.

6   Cobra pins: For our directors and suit-wearers to display.

7   Business cards: Need to be less cluttered.

8   The day in the life of a salesperson: think about this.

9   New staff tastings: So that they know the great products they are selling.

10   Invite people to tastings: Very good idea.

OUTLETS OF COBRA BEER – RETAILS AND BARS ETC

1   How to serve Cobra products: Essential knowledge; we should know and they should know.

2   Sampling of Cobra in supermarkets: A friendly, interactive event that is bound to generate excitement and new buyers!

3   Feedback form: For Cobra drinkers to tell us more.

4   Off-licence tastings with third parties: Just like supermarket tastings.

5   Recipe card: branded recipe book.

6   Business card draw: For everyone who comes into the office to drop into a bowl and then win beer for a year!

7   Housewarming/other events/Cobra contribution: A random Cobra-Beer-sponsored event.

8   Draught manual: Essential, whether for general knowledge or a salesperson in the field.

9   Tool kits: For our salespeople.

10 Cobra courier: For London deliveries to cut costs on using Ecourier.

11 Cobra hamper: With samples of all our products to give away; a standard hamper which will put an end to telesales scrambling around making boxes for Karan.

12 Uniforms for engineers: Just like the drivers.

13 Product repackaging: With branded boxes instead of normal cardboard ones.

14 Branded boxes: For product repackaging, sending out POS, sending out anything.

15 Accounts: Prompt payment.

16 New accounts/supplier booklet: So that everyone can quickly look up a reference.

COMPLAINTS

1 Company training: To deal with complaints.

2 Dealing with a complaint immediately: Needs to be stressed; the customer should know that we are courteous, interested, and prompt.

3 Form to ask the right questions: To help us.

4 How to handle a complaint: We all need to be trained to handle a complaint.

CHAPTER EIGHT

PUTTING SOMETHING BACK

On the 24 July 2006 Karan Bilimoria was formally admitted to the House of Lords. The peerage as an institution was in the media for the wrong reasons at the beginning of 2006, as the cash-for-peerages scandal hit the front pages of the press. Bilimoria, however, was appointed to the House for all the right reasons.

The Lord Bilimoria of Chelsea is a crossbencher – not appointed by a political party but elevated to the Lords by the House of Lords Appointments Commission. The commission did not cite the grounds on which he was selected, simply describing him as 'a leading young entrepreneur; founder and chief executive of Cobra Beer'. It cannot have escaped the commission's attention, however, that while Bilimoria may have built a successful business with Cobra Beer, he has also laboured behind the scenes on behalf of a host of good causes and worked on a voluntary basis for a number of public bodies.

Bilimoria's community work is partly inspired by his customers, the Indian restaurateurs; the people who have made Indian food a national way of life, if not the national cuisine of this country, who have opened up restaurants on every high street in every corner of the country.

'The Indian restaurateurs are pioneering entrepreneurs. They have gone into these areas, invariably as complete strangers, and have had to win customers, and make friends,' says Bilimoria. 'Most importantly, I have always seen them put back into the community, and engage with the community, wherever they are. I believe every business can, and should, do that in its own way.'

GIVING BACK

Initially, Bilimoria discovered that an easy way for the company to put back into the community and to help lots of initiatives was by donating its products to fundraising events. By doing so Cobra saves the organisations concerned the cost of buying drinks and simultaneously exposes its product to potential new customers.

'It is a win–win situation,' he says. 'We have been able to help hundreds of charities in this way and nowadays we are supporting some event or some charity or the other almost every day and the sums of money we are talking about now are pretty significant in terms of the value of product that we donate. So the message there is that, sure, the big cheques should continue to be written out, but there are other ways that businesses can put back into the community, no matter what their size, and one of the main ways is to donate products or services as a donation in kind.'

As the business grew, so Bilimoria got more involved with charities, including writing the cheques. One charity that benefits from Cobra's financial help, for example, is the Shrimati Pushpa Wati Loomba Memorial Trust, which educates the children of poor widows in India. In the absence of a Western-style welfare system, women whose husbands die often find themselves destitute. With an estimated 33 million widows in India, each with an average of three children, over 100 million people are affected by this predicament. Bilimoria is the chairman of the trust's advisory board and helps to organise large fundraising events.

Another example is Cobra's glass recycling operation in South Africa. Attitudes towards glass recycling differ depending on where you are in the world. In the UK there are all sorts of recycling initiatives, where glass is sorted and reprocessed in glass factories. In India, beer bottles are recycled because everyone reuses beer bottles there. There is a system where the restaurant sells the bottle to the bottle collector, who sells it to the bottle wholesaler, who sells the bottles back to the brewery. So that is the whole recycling system, and the bottles will go round fifteen times, sometimes, before they break.

In South Africa, the bottles are just thrown away. So Cobra found a shelter for homeless people in Cape Town – the Carpenter's Shop. This shelter started 25 years ago, helping homeless people by giving them accommodation and food, as well as skills training. Residents there do glasswork, carpentry and refurnishing.

Cobra collects the used beer bottles and drops them off at the shelter. There they have the machinery to shear off the tops of the bottles, round off the edges, and then they can work them into glasses. They use the 660ml bottles for serving drinks, and the 330ml bottles as candleholders. Cobra pays them the market rate of 10 rand – the same price that they sell their own bottle-glasses for at markets and fairs. The company also makes sure that it provides more bottles than it needs glasses from, which increases the personal supply of bottles for the people at the shelter, which they can later sell. The glasses are already being used in the VIP rooms of Protea Hotels, and at style bars in Cape Town.

One aspect of corporate social responsibility, of course, is the environment. With the breweries that Cobra operates, there are lots of environmental and sustainability initiatives. A good example is the brewery in India that it started doing business with in 2004. In India, power has always been a problem for industry, and there are always power shortages, so the vast majority of factories in India have their own power generating ability.

Generally they tend to be fuel-oil powered generators or coal generators. However, the brewery in Rajasthan that Cobra works with is surrounded by mustard fields. After the mustard is harvested the husk is burnt away by the farmers. So the brewery set up a plant where they bought all the waste mustard husks from the farmers, and then burnt it to generate power. It is a natural form of power, it provides income to the poor farmers, and promotes recycling. Plus it has encouraged other factories around the area to do the same thing, so everyone benefits from it.

That is not all though. Breweries throw out a lot of water. Water is used in the beer, and also for cleaning, so there is a lot of water that is left at the end of the process. Instead of just throwing that water away, the brewery treats it through an effluent plant to clean it, and then it is given to the farmers in the fields nearby, so they can use the water for irrigation.

As the scale of Cobra's giving grew, to this and other good causes, there came a point when it made sense to set up a charitable foundation and in 2006, the Cobra Foundation was born.

FIVE REASONS WHY CORPORATE SOCIAL RESPONSIBILITY IS GOOD FOR BUSINESS

- *Responsible firms attract loyal employees*: Businesses that act responsibly towards their employees and that are seen generally as responsible enjoy greater loyalty and more commitment from their staff. It is also easier to hire talent. This then shows through in dealings with customers.
- *Greater focus on environmental issues and waste reduces costs*: Firms that think about their energy consumption and use of raw materials find greater attention leads to reduced costs.
- *Responsible firms have better reputations with opinion formers and governments*: Businesses that need a licence to operate are seen as more reliable business partners and so find it easier to obtain necessary approvals.
- *Responsible firms find new ways of working and new markets*: By engaging with stakeholders, businesses see markets and opportunities in different ways and this leads to innovation.
- *Responsible firms benefit from raising capital*: Increasingly, the capital markets are examining how much management takes account of all stakeholders in their strategic planning and operations – businesses need to show that they have addressed these issues for shareholders.

Dr Lance Moir,
Director of the Centre for Financial Management, Cranfield SOM

THE COBRA FOUNDATION

A good example of Bilimoria's philosophy of doing social good through business is the Cobra Foundation. The foundation was launched on 3 March 2006, with Field Marshal Sir John Chapple and Colonel Patrick Shervington, both close friends of Bilimoria's father, as president and chairman respectively.

The foundation is the channel for the majority of Bilimoria's charitable work of which there are many examples. The General Bilimoria Fellowship, named after Bilimoria's father, provides funding for an Indian oncology specialist to travel to the UK. Nominated by an Indian cancer charity, the doctor spends three months on attachment to a British hospital conducting cancer research. The first person to travel to the UK to work in London was Surgeon Commander Ashutosh Chauhan, from the Indian Navy, who went to study at Kings College Hospital.

'It is a really important part of building a business, putting back into the community and the notion of corporate social responsibility,' says Bilimoria. 'It is not just for the sake of it, it is not for being politically correct, it actually makes sense and there are many ways in which businesses can do it.' Apart from putting company money into the Cobra Foundation, the company has launched a payroll giving scheme enabling members of the company to make voluntary donations.

KARAN'S BUSINESS TIPS:
BUSINESS – WHAT'S THE POINT?

'I find one of the most fulfilling aspects of business is the feeling that you are making a difference in everything that you are doing. So that by your being there and through your input, and as a result of your actions and your initiatives, you have taken something forward or have helped somebody,' says Bilimoria.

'So in one way being in business is a manifestation of that – making a difference, not only to your own benefit, your family's benefit, but hopefully everyone who is involved in your organisation benefits from it.

'Believe me, you are genuinely making a huge difference if your business is successful. If you think about it, everything is fuelled by business. It is business that actually creates the jobs, that makes the money, that pays the taxes, that pays for the hospitals, for schools, for defence – it all comes down to business. So you are the engine of the country. People quite often overlook that. And, of course, it's the responsibility of the country, and society's response, to create the environment for business to be able to do that. So it is a team effort, but ... we are all reliant on business.

'And then I just love the fact that I have created a product that people absolutely love. And there is no end to it because I am going to try to keep creating more and more products that people love.'

ENGAGE, ENRICH, ENJOY

One of Bilimoria's mottos in life goes like this: engage, enrich, enjoy. What does that mean? He explains it like this. To get anything out of life you have to engage. What you put in, you get out – you engage. Next, by engaging, you enrich – and are enriched; adding your experience and contributing to, as well as learning from, whatever you are doing. If you engage, you enrich, you are enriched and, most important, you enjoy. It should be fun. 'Everything I do, I genuinely enjoy. You have got to be passionate about what you are doing and you have to have fun doing it,' says Bilimoria.

In addition to his charitable work, Bilimoria has accepted a number of public appointments. Bilimoria's first appointment came in 1999 when David Blunkett, Secretary of State for Education and Employment at the time, asked him to join the New Deal taskforce. This was later renamed the National Employment Panel and switched to the Department for Work and Pensions, but Bilimoria sits on the panel to this day and was chairman of the Small and Medium Enterprise board.

Apart from his role with the National Employment Panel, Bilimoria is co-chair of the Indo British Partnership for the British Government, founder and chairman of the Indo British Partnership Network and Visiting Entrepreneur at the University of Cambridge. He is also the National Champion of the National Council for Graduate Entrepreneurship, and was the youngest university chancellor in Britain at the time of his appointment as chancellor of the Thames Valley University in May 2005.

'By engaging in public life, you are not only able to put back, but you learn so much,' he says. It may be time consuming but Bilimoria believes it is professionally worthwhile. 'All these activities I find so amazing, I learn all the time and I find them tremendously enriching.'

He believes his public appointments have not only enriched his life but have turned out to be a source of enjoyment.

EXTEND YOUR NETWORK

Business networks are an increasingly important aspect of business life. There are social/professional online networks like LinkedIn. There are networks for women such as the British Association for Women Entrepreneurs. Whatever line of business you are in, there is a network out there for you. And networks aren't just about meeting people. A lot of recent research, conducted by organisations such as the Advanced Institute of Management Research in UK, for example, suggest that networks are a route to innovation and competitive advantage.

Bilimoria is an active member of a number of business networks. In fact he describes joining one particular network – the Young Presidents' Organisation (YPO) – as one of the best things he has ever done.

The YPO motto is 'Better leaders through education and idea exchange', and that is the key to belonging to the YPO. Attending YPO events is about continual learning. Bilimoria finds the peer group idea exchange and learning an invaluable source of help for his business life.

'Once a month I meet with my forum group of ten people based in London, and we are all peers in different industries, often from different countries and different businesses; some are entrepreneurs, some are chief execs, some run family businesses,' says Bilimoria. 'They are running businesses from billion pound businesses to smaller businesses. Every month we get together and help each other and coach each other.'

Bilimoria believes activities such as these are extremely useful for entrepreneurs and other managing executives. The more help you can get from people who are independent, who have no vested interest other than to help

THE YOUNG PRESIDENTS' ORGANIZATION

The Young Presidents' Organization (YPO) was founded in New York in 1950. It is now a global organisation with over 9500 global business leaders in more than 75 countries. Members rely on an exclusive peer network that connects them to exchange ideas, pursue learning and share strategies to achieve personal and professional growth and success.

The mission of the Young Presidents' Organization is to create *better leaders through education and idea exchange*.

www.ypo.org

KARAN'S BUSINESS TIPS: INTERNSHIPS

One unexpected benefit from Bilimoria's relationship with the business schools is the internship programme that runs at Cobra from March to September.

The company has taken in students from Harvard Business School, London Business School, Cambridge University, and Cranfield School of Management, and many other universities and schools in Britain. Interns join either on an individual basis, or as a team on a project on Cobra – which they are assessed on. This arrangement benefits both student and company, with the intern getting to experience how a dynamic, successful business operates from close quarters, while Cobra gets some of the brightest business minds looking at operational issues, product development or some other aspect of the business. Every intern is a breath of fresh air for the company, says Bilimoria.

you, and that can stand back, and view your business in an objective and impartial way, the better, says Bilimoria.

CONTINUAL LEARNING

Another activity that Bilimoria engages in outside the business is executive education, primarily through business schools. It started at a time when he was at a critical growth phase with the business. A faculty member at Cranfield School of Management, one of the UK's leading business schools, met Bilimoria during a fund-raising exercise and sent him a brochure for the Business Growth Programme at Cranfield. Bilimoria, who had seriously considered taking an MBA at Harvard Business School, but had eventually opted for a law degree at Cambridge, jumped at the chance to do what was effectively a mini MBA.

Bilimoria views the course at Cranfield as a turning point in his business life. Not only did it give him contacts at the school that subsequently provided some very sound business advice regarding Cobra, but it also gave him other opportunities. As he became more involved with the business schools it was a natural progression to start lecturing. Since then Bilimoria has lectured at a number of leading business schools including Cranfield, Harvard and London Business School. He is the Visiting Entrepreneur at Cambridge. It is not just the students at the business schools who benefit from this. Bilimoria finds the process of preparing for his lectures and being quizzed by students about his views is an educational process for him as well.

KARAN'S BUSINESS TIPS:
LIFELONG LEARNING

'Every single person, whatever capacity they work in life, can say, "I'm too busy, I have no time." But you have to make the time. It is often an effort to make that time, and an expense to go on these courses. But you are reaching out, you are engaging. You are being outward looking, and this is very important. The trap in growing a business as an entrepreneur is that it is so easy to get caught up in your own business and become insular and inward looking.

'The advantage in being outward looking and reaching out is so, so crucial, and so beneficial. If you go and attend a course at a business school regularly, for one, you are getting away from your business and that stepping aside in itself is beneficial. You are meeting with other business people, so you are learning from each other and each other's experiences and you are learning from whatever is on the course.

'More often than not, I find that when I come back from these courses, not only do I come back refreshed and invigorated, but I come up with huge amounts – lists – of ideas, that I come back and share with my team. And many of them have been major initiatives within the company, all as a result of attending these courses.

'I am often asked: do you have any regrets, have you made any mistakes? And the biggest mistake I made, the biggest regret I have – I try not to regret much but I do have one regret – is that I did not discover the value of lifelong learning until 1998 when I went on the Cranfield course.'

Despite the tremendous success of Cobra, and the fact that Bilimoria is lecturing other executives and future business leaders, Bilimoria's own journey of lifelong learning continues. He has returned to Cranfield for refresher courses and now attends a Harvard Business School week-long course that runs every year for a week, as well as the Young Presidents' Organization one-week course that he founded and runs at London Business School. No matter how busy he is, he always makes time for these programmes.

At Cobra lifelong learning is not just for the boss. A culture of lifelong learning is engrained in the company. The company's management team regularly take courses. The marketing director, for example, completed a

EXECUTIVE EDUCATION

For many executives, taking a standard MBA programme is not a realistic option. Usually they are too busy to take lengthy periods away from work. Senior executives, even the successful ones, still need to update and refresh their knowledge and skills, however. Luckily for time-hungry executives, business schools provide a number of time saving options.

Executive education is, unsurprisingly, aimed at executives, rather than graduates without work experience. It comes in two types: non-degree and executive MBA (EMBA).

Non-degree courses may be open courses, available to any executives that wish to apply, or custom courses tailored to fit the needs of an individual company. They can last for anything from a day to several weeks, and there are courses that cover a range of business disciplines or those that focus on specific areas.

Exec-ed is usually associated with more senior levels of management, although most schools have programmes for different career stages; ages range from late 20s to mid 50s, with an average around 40.

Business school flagship executive education programmes include the Advanced Management Programmes at Harvard Business School in the US and INSEAD at Fontainebleau in France, the Stanford Executive Programme at Stanford Graduate School of Business in the US, London Business School's Senior Executive Programme and Cranfield's Business Growth Programme.

Masters in marketing studying part-time at Kingston, one of the top marketing universities, while working at Cobra. Not only did he get a qualification out of it, he was able to put into practice what he learnt, so Cobra also benefited.

GETTING THE BALANCE RIGHT

Combining all the external activities plus running a business with a healthy family life is no easy task yet Bilimoria seems to square the circle effortlessly. He will tell you, however, that as easy as it appears, it can be very tough at times. For others struggling to find balance he offers some pointers.

Bilimoria says there is much truth in the saying: 'If you want something done, ask a busy person.' Busy people seem to get things done. Why? One of the reasons is that they prioritise. If it is important enough, then you make the time for it.

Secondly, says Bilimoria, you need very supportive friends and family. Bilimoria is lucky to the extent that he lives just five minutes away from his office, which means he can pop into the house for five minutes in between meetings or, if he has an evening function to attend, he will stop at the house for half an hour in between leaving the office and going to the function.

He also believes in extended family trips; but not in the separation of work and personal life. In the modern world the trick is managing and balancing the two together, rather than separately, blending work, family life and external activities in a way that works best for everyone involved.

As an entrepreneur running his own business, Bilimoria is able to control his own timetable to some extent. 'You don't have to be somewhere at nine, or somewhere at five, you can be flexible with your time,' he says. 'And now, with communications the way they are, you can work from anywhere in the world.'

In Bilimoria's case, anywhere in the world often means South Africa or India. He is keen that his children are aware of the family heritage and history. Every year the family Bilimoria makes a three or four week trip to South Africa, where his wife comes from, as well as a similar length trip to India. These are not 'full-time holidays' however: Bilimoria will inevitably get some work done at the same time. In India in early 2006, for example, he took the opportunity to visit the Cobra office in Mumbai and also fulfilled a number of speaking engagements.

The third ingredient to finding the fulcrum for family–work balance is support within the workplace. As with most busy business people there came a point – in Bilimoria's case a few years ago – when he found himself struggling to juggle all the elements of his life. It was then that he met a successful businessman who, like himself, was heavily involved in charitable work. The businessman asked Bilimoria how many PAs he had. The answer: one. The businessman on the other hand had three and suggested that Bilimoria step up his internal support team. 'He was absolutely right,' Bilimoria says. 'Today I have a team of six!'

CHAPTER NINE

WHEN THE GOING GETS TOUGH

Business doesn't always run smoothly, as any entrepreneur will tell you. All businesses face crises from time to time. Some small, some potentially business busting. Major corporate crises, such as the Exxon Valdez oil spill, the Perrier benzene contamination, or the Tylenol product tampering should be a lesson for all organisations large and small. Take the example of Perrier. In 1990 it was reported that traces of benzene had been discovered in Perrier's bottled water. The company was slow to react to the crisis. Sales dived. Over the next three years the company lost substantial market share.

There is an important lesson here for organisations. The way that a company reacts to a crisis is crucial. The key is preparation. It is important to think the unthinkable and then plan for it. It is a lesson that Bilimoria learnt the hard way.

WHOEVER SAID THERE'S NO SUCH THING AS BAD PUBLICITY?

Bilimoria will never forget 19 February 1998. It was the day that Iqbal Wahhab rushed into his office waving a copy of the latest issue of *Tandoori* magazine.

Once located in the Cobra offices, Wahhab and the magazine had since moved into accommodation of its own across a courtyard. Bilimoria remained the de facto publisher and a minority shareholder, with Cobra as an advertiser; however he had very little to do with the magazine on a day-to-day basis. He certainly didn't proof the contents of the magazine before it went to press – and that was as true for the issue Wahhab was waving as any other. Bilimoria hadn't even seen this issue. It wasn't long before he wished that he had though.

The magazine was all over the national press because of a leader Wahhab had written which criticised standards of service in Indian restaurants. And all the newspapers had picked up on the particularly trenchant phrase Wahhab had used to describe the waiters themselves.

As Bilimoria digested the article that had attracted all the media attention, he was consumed by a sense of impending doom. 'I remember reading the article and thinking, "Oh dear, I don't like the way things have been expressed here".'

Bilimoria's editorial instincts proved well-founded. It soon became clear that the article's consequences would be of disastrous proportions. As Wahhab's comments sunk in, the magazine's readers, mostly the Indian restaurant owners and other people in the Indian restaurant trade, reacted with fury. Soon, copies of *Tandoori* were being burned in the street and Wahhab was receiving death threats.

It didn't stop there. Groups of restaurateurs held meetings to discuss how to respond to the perceived assault on their standards. *Tandoori* was a free magazine, and so it was not possible for the restaurant to stop the magazine from being published. But going after one of the owners and the publisher of the magazine was another matter. And so it was that Cobra found itself on the receiving end of a boycott of its beer brand by two restaurant associations, representing hundreds of restaurants.

'It was completely unfair, because Cobra had nothing to do with it,' says Bilimoria. 'I didn't even know the article had been written. But no one was willing to listen to me.'

Bilimoria moved quickly. Wahhab resigned and Bilimoria – as publisher of the magazine – made a formal apology. The next issue of *Tandoori* ran more than 2000 words of apology over four pages. But the damage was done. The anger of the *Tandoori* readers was not sated. Cobra sales plummeted. Up until this point, the company's growth rate had been running at 70 per cent per annum. The year before, sales had doubled. Now it was facing a meltdown as an extremely disciplined boycott took effect.

It couldn't have come at a worse time. 'We had a world class product, world class packaging, Cobra on draught, newly designed fonts, and great point of sale,' says Bilimoria. 'We had raised some money, we had our financing and invoice discounting facilities in place, the brand was getting more and more popular, and for the first time we had appointed an advertising agency, Team Saatchi, one of the best agencies in the world.'

The Curryholic Dave advertising campaign was underway and due to run over the whole of the spring, and then again in the summer if the initial burst of advertising proved effective. In support of the predicted sales surge, Cobra opened depots in Manchester and Leeds as part of a plan to create a national network allowing it to deliver directly to restaurants in addition to using distributors. Meanwhile, Cobra's chief executive had been honing his business skills on the Business Growth Programme at Cranfield School of Management, one of the best business schools in Europe. Everything was fabulous.

In the wake of the article, however, this rosy picture evaporated overnight. Cobra's PR company had never dealt with anything like it before and was at a loss over how to combat the company's detractors. No one had legislated for the possibility that the editor of *Tandoori* magazine would write something that offended the whole industry, leading to a well-organised boycott of Cobra beer.

As Bilimoria says: 'If you have a strike at least you have the option of trying to get your production done somewhere else, or of trying to bring in some other staff, but when your own customers refuse to buy from you – that has to be one of the worst scenarios.'

Soon Cobra was feeling the financial strain. Apart from the £350,000 it had invested in its advertising campaign, there was the cost of setting up the depots as well as the recruitment drive.

When Bilimoria got in contact with the company's bankers he discovered that Cobra's account had been transferred from the care of the helpful manager that Cobra enjoyed an excellent relationship with, to a special division

KEY ELEMENTS OF CRISIS MANAGEMENT:

- *It WILL happen to you*: Whatever your organisation does, at some point it will be embroiled in a crisis – sometimes not even of your own making or fault. You must (as a matter of basic governance) prepare now – reacting on the day is usually suicidal – think Union Carbide Bhopal.
- *Perception IS reality*: Even if you are squeaky clean/right/moral etc., if the public/media perceive you as the bad guy then you will be! You must be totally proactive in putting over your side of the argument and realise that many people will be behaving emotionally and not rationally – think Shell Brent Spar.
- *Crisis CAN be opportunity:* If you prepare for and then manage a crisis well you can even enhance your organisation's image – think Johnson & Johnson Tylenol.
- *Regret. Reason. Remedy:* Show the public that you are human – show regret (don't worry, you are not legally apologising). Then do your best to explain what has happened and give some 'remedy/positive traction' to the story that shows that you are dealing with it.
- *Don't panic:* Fear is the mind killer. Everyone will be shouting at you, 'experts' will be giving you contrary advice and many of your team will be punch drunk and irrational within minutes. Agree your position, communicate it clearly and don't be lead into the 'killing fields' of rumour and conjecture. If you can keep your head ...
- *Oh and one other*: Prepare, prepare, train, train, rehearse, rehearse.

Stephen Carver, Cranfield School of Management

of the bank. 'We were told it was "an intensive care unit" where the bank could look after us better,' says Bilimoria. 'It turned out to be a unit where they put companies into receivership and administration.'

At that stage the bank was exposed to the tune of £60,000. Bilimoria was told to stick to the overdraft limit, and the £135,000 duty deferment facility, agreed with the bank some time before, was withdrawn.

Despite the bad news the bank did give one useful piece of advice, suggesting that Cobra approach an insurance company to obtain a deferment guarantee. Bilimoria discovered that insurance companies were prepared to offer bigger guarantees at more competitive rates, useful information that he still uses to good effect.

TROUBLE BREWING

At about the same time, the company was hit by another financial blow. John Wells, managing director of brewing firm Charles Wells, retired and was replaced by a younger member of the family, Paul Wells.

Charles Wells' strategy had put growth before profit, boosting the turnover to £100 million, but with profits languishing at £1 million. Paul Wells, then in his early forties, adopted a different strategy. At that stage it was one of the largest – if not the largest – contract brewers of own-brand beers in the country. Several of the major supermarkets' own label beers, lagers and ales were brewed by the firm. Paul Wells intended to exit this low margin business and focus instead on Charles Wells-branded products. Acknowledging that Cobra had potential, the Charles Wells brewery agreed to continue brewing Cobra lager-beer, but only on condition that Bilimoria accepted a whopping 25 per cent hike in the brewing price.

Cobra was in the course of a five-year contract at this time. Bilimoria had little choice but to accept.

Paul Wells was under pressure from his family to perform. Had John Wells still been in charge then Bilimoria, drawing on their long-standing relationship, might have been able to negotiate a better deal for Cobra. But at the time there was no such relationship with the younger Wells. As it turns out, the new strategic direction taken by Paul Wells paid off. Following an initial slump in turnover caused by the move out of supermarket brewing, the brewing firm's turnover is now back above £100 million and its profitability is much improved.

That said, the hawkish attitude of Cobra's bankers and the price hike from Charles Wells meant that costs at Cobra had to be cut. While all this was happening, Cobra's business was under the scrutiny of a team of MBA students from Cranfield – a service the business school offered all the executives who took Bilimoria's particular course.

In the event it was a lucky coincidence. One of the team's key recommendations was to abandon the new depot strategy. The Cranfield team thought that Cobra's expansion plans were too ambitious at that point. With the boycott ongoing, the Cranfield team recommended that Cobra shut down its depots, which were burning money and taking up valuable management time, to fight fires elsewhere. 'It was a really, really tough decision to make,' says Bilimoria. 'We did it though, we cut the depots.'

Bilimoria also had to go through the trauma of firing his first marketing manager. Julia Minchin had moved to the country to start a family. In her place, after 'a major recruitment process', he had hired Simon Edwards, a top-flight marketing man from Courage. Within a month of him joining in the summer of 1998, however, Bilimoria was telling him he was going to have to let him go, in a bid to cut overheads. It didn't make it any easier that Edwards was just about to get married at the time.

'It was such a difficult decision to make,' says Bilimoria. 'I remember going home and crying – and I very rarely cry. I said to myself, how can I do this to such a wonderful chap, who we had recruited with great difficulty, all because of a situation that Cobra was not responsible for?' To ease the pain Bilimoria told Edwards that he didn't have to leave straight away, and could work his month's notice if he wished. As events turned out, Bilimoria managed to keep him on somehow. He was still working for the company in 2006 – as marketing director.

A SILVER LINING

The *Tandoori* incident could have sunk the company. Eventually, however, what started off as a company threatening crisis turned out to have some unexpected benefits. At the time it might not have seemed like it, but the company emerged a better company for its experiences.

As so many of Cobra's activities were outsourced, from manufacturing to distribution, it managed to cut its overheads in half, and not just by a reduction in its own headcount. In the process, marketing expenditure was reduced to virtually nil in the wake of the advertising campaign, and the company's debt bill was attacked aggressively.

'We cut out lots of overheads, so we actually became a much leaner company,' says Bilimoria. 'The flexibility made the difference between us surviving or not. Then once the boycott was lifted, that same flexibility enabled us to gear up very quickly.'

In times of crisis it soon becomes apparent who are the people you can rely on. Cobra's predicament was eased by the understanding shown by some key associates. The invoice finance company allowed Cobra to go beyond its 85 per cent drawdown on its debtors. At Grant Thornton, Anuj Chande offered to approach some existing shareholders to see if there was anything they could do to help.

Bilimoria was keen to hang onto his shares, having diluted his holding down to 72 per cent at the end of 1995. The last thing he wanted to do was sell more shares in a distress situation. He knew the value would be way below the shares' true worth.

So Chande spoke to Pierre Brahm, who said he was willing to raise cash on one of his properties and lend the money to the company. Another shareholder, Geoff Ho, said his primary residence in London was unmortgaged and he was willing to raise money on that and lend it to Cobra.

'By then, we'd known Pierre Brahm since 1993, so we had known him four years, and he had become a good friend,' says Bilimoria. 'I had barely known Geoff Ho for two years, but he had already become a friend. It just shows you there are the people who you can depend on, who are willing to put their own necks on the line for you. And I will never forget that.' It just goes to show how even in times of crisis help can come from unexpected places.

As it turned out, Bilimoria didn't need to borrow from either Brahm or Ho. This was largely due to the efforts of Jaimin Chandarana, then Cobra's chief accountant and today its financial controller, plus the efforts of the sales team. Chandarana juggled creditors and pleaded with suppliers for more time to pay, while the sales force worked on the restaurateurs, banging home the message that Cobra was innocent. Samson Sohail, Cobra's sales director in charge of restaurants, drove thousands of miles up and down the country lobbying restaurant owners and arranging face-to-face meetings between his boss and restaurateurs whose loyalty to the boycott was wavering. Sohail also took out a personal loan of £50,000 from his private bankers and loaned the money to the company – an act of complete and utter loyalty.

In a situation like this, you should take every opportunity to communicate your message to the customers. Bilimoria did just that. 'I remember getting a phone call from Samson at 10.30pm, telling me there were some restaurateurs in Bath ready to meet with us and discuss the situation,' says Bilimoria. 'I put on a jacket and tie, Samson picked me up, and we drove down from London to Bath. We got there at about 12.30am and we were in a meeting with these restaurant owners there until three in the morning.'

Sohail had got together the owners of five key influencing restaurants in the area. After hearing Bilimoria's side of the story they agreed to start stocking Cobra once again. These midnight PR missions became a common part of Bilimoria's routine at the time.

Towards the end of 1998, significant cracks were beginning to appear in the restaurateurs' previously united front. Some restaurateurs would stop short of putting Cobra back on the menu, but would keep some in stock to serve to customers who requested it. Others simply broke ranks. Cobra's charm offensive, coupled with the fact that Wahhab had initiated libel proceedings against one of the restaurant associations which had allegedly made some defamatory remarks about him, was having its effect. The boycott was officially withdrawn in March 1999, just over a year after it had begun. Almost immediately, orders returned to their pre-boycott level.

In 1999–2000, sales of Cobra shot up by 50 per cent. Even more impressive in its own way, however, is the fact that sales in the year of the boycott did not dip: instead they grew by three per cent. Although the £350,000 spent on Curryholic Dave was a strain given the events, it was one of the main factors that kept the company from going under during the boycott. It helped reinforce the strength of an increasingly popular brand. It is a great case for the benefits of a decent marketing budget.

A CRISIS RESOLVED

Not all crises end as well. Bilimoria reacted in the right way, and he was lucky. In the *Tandoori* tale the nice guys didn't finish last. Wahhab, who honourably fell on his sword, losing the putative restaurant business he was working on at the time the *Tandoori* article was published, went on to become a successful

KARAN'S BUSINESS TIPS:
COMMUNICATION DURING A CRISIS.

'There may be times, especially during a crisis, when you can't pay people, because of the predicament you are in,' says Bilimoria. 'Then it is really important to communicate constantly with everyone, always let people know what is going on, and say if you can't do something. Wherever possible, pay small amounts if you can and let people see some movement and then reassure them that there are open lines of communication. And then make sure that you don't let them down and you pay every penny.'

During the boycott Cobra owed Saatchi a huge amount of money for the advertising campaign, Bilimoria had to pay them, but obviously the situation was very difficult for the company. Bilimoria was completely open with his contacts at Saatchi about the situation. Fortunately they were very supportive. They understood Cobra's position and gave the company time to get the money together.

'At the end of it all, in a situation like this, it's all about people trusting you. They will usually be prepared to accept that it may be a slow pay, as long as it is a sure pay,' says Bilimoria. 'Of course, in the end we left nobody out. We paid every single person, and that is how you get support in times of trouble – by having that communication.'

restaurateur, founding the hugely impressive and popular Cinnamon Club in Westminster, and now runs a critically acclaimed restaurant in London's Borough Market called Roast.

Bilimoria's 'nasty' banker, meanwhile, was fired by him the moment things returned to normal and Bilimoria found 'a wonderful person' at one of its competitors.

The crisis over, Bilimoria made a graceful exit from *Tandoori*, selling his 45 per cent stake to the remaining shareholders in 2003. Despite the trauma he went through because of his involvement in it, he remains proud of its achievements.

'We created something that has been a huge benefit to the whole industry,' he says. 'Before *Tandoori*, there was no high quality publication that went out on a regular basis, month after month, nowadays quarter after quarter, to the restaurants. It gives them information, helps them to communicate with each other, and helps suppliers to communicate with them. All free of charge.'

THREATS TO OPPORTUNITIES

Bilimoria likes to say that, invariably, threats are opportunities. It sounds like one of those catchy managerial aphorisms, but Bilimoria speaks from experience.

Chapter Seven detailed how, a couple of times each year, Bilimoria and the senior management team leave behind the hurly-burly of everyday business life and escape to contemplate strategy, and indulge in some scenario planning.

It was at one such retreat, held at Christopher Edgcumbe-Rendle's London pied-à-terre in Battersea, southwest London, that the idea for one of the company's successful new products came about – although few of the team that attended that meeting would have predicted it.

At the time, the beginning of 1999, an invasion of Iraq looked imminent. Bilimoria and his team were mulling over the consequences of such an invasion. Would the Middle East descend into chaos? Would it trigger a global recession? How would it impact on Cobra's business? In the middle of this exploration of the shifts in global geopolitical power, Edgcumbe-Rendle put his hand up and said: 'Stop, stop, I've thought of a major threat to the business – wine.'

PAT CHAPMAN: EMINENT FOOD CRITIC, JOURNALIST, AUTHOR OF THE *COBRA GOOD CURRY GUIDE*

What is your connection with Karan Bilimoria and Cobra Beer?
When Karan first asked if he could meet me in 1990 and enquired how we might work together, I offered him sponsorship of the renowned *Cobra Good Curry Guide*. It comes out every three years, and six editions (and 16 years) later, Cobra is still the sponsor. When Karan and Iqbal started *Tandoori* magazine, I offered help by way of database information and as a contributing editor to the magazine, a role I still hold.

What makes Cobra special as a business?

On the face of it, in 1990 when Cobra started, anyone would say selling beer to the British was a non-starter. Many did say that; I believe some of his family said it! I was dubious myself, but how clever to use the Indian restaurants as his opening gambit. I would have invested in the business had I been asked; I was never asked, but from that first meeting, I have always believed in Karan. Karan's contemporary marketing statements say it all (the story on the bottle). Karan has proved that a real company can come from nowhere and with clever marketing get on the road to become a world-class, worldwide blue-chip brand. Once past the self-delivery stage from the back of his car, he has used only top marketing, PR and advertising agencies, and his products and packaging are now as good as any.

What aspect of the Cobra business would you hold up as best practice to other entrepreneurs and business owners?

Karan is loyal to his Cobra staff. Few have left his employ over the years. He is also loyal to people like me. A handshake is a contract with Karan. He requires the best from everyone, including himself. But he can make the tough decisions. A good example of that was his decision to stop using his Indian bottler (Mysore Breweries Bangalore) which surprised me and many others, including the bottler, whom I know really well thanks to Cobra. But the decision proved to be sound. It enabled Karan to achieve much higher quality of bottles and packaging.

Could you recall one memory or story of your experiences with Cobra that defines the Karan Bilimoria and Cobra approach to business?

Any history of Cobra/Karan cannot omit the infamous boycott episode. During the period that Iqbal Wahhab was editor of *Tandoori* magazine, he asked me to write what he called a Rage Page, where industry matters that annoyed me could be aired. It was always intended to offer advice to restaurateurs. Sometimes Iqbal wrote the piece and it was the restaurant service piece that led to Iqbal's resignation and a seriously bad patch for Cobra, where many restaurants boycotted the products.

Karan asked for my help several times with long phone calls in the weeks that followed and I wrote several pieces to try rectify the situation. The business was approaching near-collapse, but Karan persevered and the recovery occurred. I know Karan has never forgotten the help and support I gave, little though it was. But it shows how volatile the market is and above all, it was a big test of Karan's resolve.

The immediate reaction of the group was: 'Wake up, Chris, we're a beer company, don't talk about wine'. But then Edgcumbe-Rendle pointed out that more and more people were drinking wine generally, and more and more people were drinking wine with Indian food in Indian restaurants, and therefore they were going to drink less beer.

There was a moment's silence as the group digested the information and it dawned on them that maybe Edgcumbe-Rendle was right. Wine was a threat, and they needed to come up with a response. Their first reaction was to work out how to persuade the wine drinkers to drink beer. But they soon realised that approach was a waste of time. 'You can't tell the customer what to drink,' says Bilimoria.

The team decided to go away and investigate the threat, before deciding what strategy to adopt to deal with it. The results of the research were worrying; the situation was even worse than they had imagined. Huge quantities of wine were being consumed in Indian restaurants: no less than 20 per cent of customers drinking in Indian restaurants were drinking wine. The only positive aspect of the research, from Cobra's point of view, was that 50 per cent of the wine sold was house wine – and fairly cheap table wine too, they suspected. Little attention appeared to be paid to the vintage, the variety, or the brand. In most cases, the house wine was the cheapest kind of table wine on the market.

This wasn't true of all restaurants though. In good quality mainstream restaurant groups, Conran for example, the house wines may have been the lowest priced wines on the list, but they were wines the restaurants were proud to serve as a house wine. So why didn't every Indian restaurant have wines of this quality as house wines?

VINTAGE BILIMORIA

In true Bilimoria fashion, having spotted an opportunity he went all out to exploit it. Cobra would launch its own brand of wine: a premium house wine by the standards of the sector, but still affordable.

But this was only half the battle. It wasn't enough to find a good wine. As with Cobra beer the main challenge was to find a wine that would go well with Indian food. Unsurprisingly everyone had an opinion, including the wine critics. The rise in popularity of the Indian restaurant meant that the UK was blessed with a variety of Indian restaurants, including a select group of award-winning high quality restaurants which were beginning to serve fine wines with their cuisine.

Pairing wines with Indian dishes was a popular pastime with the wine critics. 'People would say, for example, that with a korma you need a good sauvignon,' says Bilimoria. 'With a rogan josh, you need a full-bodied claret, and so on.'

Bilimoria considered this approach but decided that while it was a nice theory, and a good topic of conversation, it was not very practical. The reality was that diners in an Indian restaurant order lots of different dishes for the table, and people share the food. Plus the dishes are likely to be extremely varied in taste and texture. There are breads and rices, dahls, tandoori dishes, curries, biryanis – all these different flavours and textures, some mild, some spicy. Attempting to match each dish with a different wine, would result in more wine glasses on the table than plates of food.

A team of three Cobra executives, Bilimoria, Edwards, and Edgcumbe-Rendle, embarked on the search for one red and one white wine which would work with a wide range of Indian dishes. The criteria were that the wines should be easy drinking wines, with no sharp edges, and able to accompany a range of flavours. Plus, while they would be excellent value for money, they would also subscribe to the Cobra ethos of being a premium product.

Having already licensed the brewing of Cobra beer, Bilimoria wasn't about to become a vintner, however. His idea was to approach various wine growers around the world, identify a suitable supplier, or suppliers, and then produce a suitable product. Thanks to Cobra's status as an established beer brand, with extensive sales and marketing expertise and a customer base of 6000 Indian restaurants, vineyards were eager to get involved.

There followed a marathon sampling as the team tasted over 400 wines. The exercise ended with the selection of a well-known winemaker called Paul Buitolot who was half French and half British. 'We chose the Languedoc region in the south of France, which is the largest wine producing area in the world,' says Bilimoria. 'There are more wines produced in the Languedoc than in the whole of Australia or California.'

KARAN'S BUSINESS TIPS: DIFFERENT PRODUCTS, DIFFERENT APPROACHES.

'If you have one success-ful product and plan to launch another don't expect that the same branding approach will automatically work, says Bilimoria.

'I was delighted by the idea of naming our wine after my father, but I made a mistake with the first attempt at branding, when the wines were launched in November 1999,' he says. 'It was called General Bil-ly's. It had a very bright, metallic label and people didn't take it seriously. You can't necessarily apply beer marketing and beer mes-sages to wine, they're dif-ferent. We realised we had to be flexible and adaptable and listen to the customer. Within six months we had changed it to the much more traditional "General Bilimoria", and embla-zoned it with my father's crest. Sales took off.'

After much debate, Cobra's team settled on a blend of Terret and Sauvignon as the white and a Merlot as the red. The next step was choosing a brand name. Calling it Cobra just didn't feel right – it was too closely associated with beer in the mind of the consumer.

It was Team Saatchi who eventually came up with the name. Because of the close relationship the Cobra creative team at Saatchi had developed with Cobra's founder they were aware that his father had been an oenophile, (a lover of wine), since his earli-est days as a soldier. His regiment of Gurkhas had inherited some fine French wines from the British, and on all formal occasions toasts were drunk with wine. As he had drunk wine with Indian food for so long, the general had often told his son that he should sell wine. Why not name the wine after his father, Team Saatchi suggested to Bilimoria.

As with Cobra's beer production Bilimoria was keen to spread the production risk. It wasn't long before the General Bilimoria wine brand was extended with the addition of another wine producer from the Languedoc near Carcassone, called St Oriel.

The next step was to look further afield. First one of South Africa's leading wine makers, then Spain where wines were sourced from a vineyard near Valencia. Today, the General Bilimoria range con-sists of ten wines, including Merlot, Terret Sauvi-gnon and Grenache Syrah from France; Pinotage, Colombard-Chardonnay, Chenin Blanc and Shiraz-Pinotage from South Africa; and Tempranillo and dry Muscat from Spain. (The Tempranillo won a silver medal at the 2005 Monde Selection Awards.)

'The beauty of this arrangement is that if a vintage is very bad in one area, we don't have to buy the wines from that area,' says Bilimoria. 'We have

never had to do that to date, but in a downside scenario we have the flexibility to bring in more Spanish or more South African if the French is not
good one year.'

Today, more than 325,000 bottles of General Bilimoria are sold each year,
with ten per cent of that total exported to the US, India and South Africa. As
the Indian restaurant market accounts for around a million cases of wine a
year, Cobra has three per cent of the market, an impressive achievement for
a brand that is only a little more than six years old. There is scope for growth
as the wines are sold in only 1000 Indian restaurants and not all restaurants
take the entire range. Many take just one red and one white.

The General Bilimoria products account for just a tiny percentage of
Cobra's turnover but they have a soft benefit for Cobra too as they use the
same distribution channels. 'Every time the wine is talked about, they talk
about the beer too, so they cross promote each other as well,' explains Bilimoria. 'It is an example of turning a threat into an opportunity.

CHAPTER TEN

GOING GLOBAL

Some of Bilimoria's best ideas come to him when he is 30,000 feet above ground, flying around the world on business. And so it was with the Grand Canyon plan. Flying across the US in 2003, Bilimoria was thinking about the business. More importantly he was considering the question: Where do I want Cobra to be in 10 years time? As the plane flew over the Grand Canyon, Bilimoria jotted down the answer: by 2014 Cobra would be a billion dollar retail value brand.

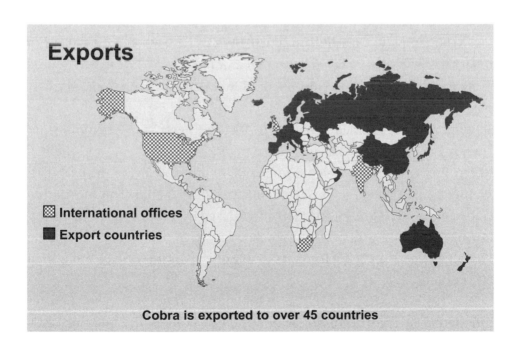

Exports

⊠ **International offices**
■ **Export countries**

Cobra is exported to over 45 countries

That was some ambition. The company was a long way from that target at the time, (even in 2006 Cobra was a $175m retail value brand, leaving some way to go).

'We always express ourselves in retail value, because that is how the consumer can identify with it,' he says. 'I set 2014 as a target and so we need to grow by six times in the next eight years. We have grown nearly eight times in the last eight years, so I think we can grow six times in the next eight years.'

To achieve such stratospheric growth, Bilimoria knew that Cobra would have to break out of the Indian restaurant market, move into the mainstream, and become a global brand to rival the majors. The success of the Curryholic Dave campaign had in some ways pushed Cobra into a corner. Cobra beer was seen as the best beer to drink with Indian food, but not on its own.

The challenge was to boost sales of Cobra as a stand-alone drink through supermarkets and pubs, bars and night clubs, without alienating the brand's existing client base. The company had already hired SHS Sales and Marketing in October 2002 – a company which specialises in selling products such as Tropicana and WKD to the on-trade. The thinking was that Cobra did not have the expertise or the personnel to attack the mainstream market itself and SHS had performed brilliantly with WKD, which achieved £250m of retail sales in 2003, just seven years after launch.

By partnering with specialist talent, Bilimoria was giving Cobra the best possible chance to succeed in developing this new market. By the end of September 2004, SHS had signed up JD Wetherspoon, Wolverhampton and Dudley Breweries, Mitchell and Butler, Yates's, Eldridge Pope, and the Belhaven Brewery; the most significant of these probably being the deal with Wetherspoon's, which stocks Cobra in 570 of its 650 pubs. This meant that Cobra was available to 4500 outlets and stocked by 1200 of them. In the following 12 months, Cobra went from being listed in 630 outlets – excluding Wetherspoon's – to being listed in 1930 outlets, an increase of more than 200 per cent.

Alongside the efforts of SHS, Cobra built up a significant mainstream sales function of its own, beginning with a team dedicated to selling into independent bars and clubs. In September 2005, the team grew from two to nine, and was responsible for almost a third of the new listings.

In the same way, Cobra created a sales force of five people dedicated to the non-supermarket. The hiring of a national accounts controller to sell into both national and regional brewers completed the in-house line up. By January 2006, the mainstream sales teams were doing so well that Cobra decided to take its sales function back in-house.

Today you can find Cobra's products just about everywhere you can buy beer. Supermarket chains stocking Cobra include Safeway, Tesco, Sainsbury's, Waitrose, Morrisons, Asda, Somerfield and Budgens. In addition to the Indian restaurants that offer Cobra, it is available in the off-licence sector, where Thresher's, Bargain Booze, Wine Rack, Bottom's Up, Costco, Victoria Wine and Unwins all sell Cobra. Meanwhile, Virgin Atlantic, Jet Airways and Air India serve it on their flights. Mainstream sales of Cobra exceeded sales to Indian restaurants for the first time in 2006.

This rapid growth, in such a relatively short space of time, bodes well for Cobra. And there is still plenty of scope for increasing sales to the company's core customers. Cobra bottled beer has already achieved substantial penetration in the Indian restaurant market. Of the 8800 or so Indian restaurants in the UK, some 6000 are licensed. Of these, Cobra bottled beer is on sale in 5400 of them – 90 per cent. Cobra draught, however, is sold in only 38 per cent of licensed Indian restaurants in the UK.

Your first instinct might tell you that selling draught Cobra to a restaurant that is already stocking bottled Cobra will cannibalise bottle sales, possibly damaging the brand of the bottled version, while not making any appreciable difference to revenue growth. In fact there is very little cannibalisation between the two products.

'We subsequently realised, through experience, that somebody who likes draught lager will drink draught lager, and somebody who likes bottled lager will drink bottled lager,' says Bilimoria. 'We discovered that when we put the two side by side, our overall sales doubled, because there is very little crossover in terms of cannibalisation. Now we can't put in the draught installations quickly enough.'

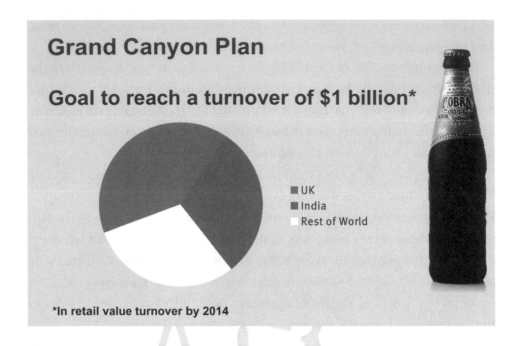

Grand Canyon Plan

Goal to reach a turnover of $1 billion*

- UK
- India
- Rest of World

*In retail value turnover by 2014

THE INDIA CHALLENGE

While domestic sales are helping Bilimoria edge towards his Grand Canyon ambitions, to get anywhere the billion dollar mark Cobra will need to be firmly established as an international brand and not just a domestic UK brand.

At the time he was winging his way over the Nevada desert in 2003, Bilimoria had already committed to global expansion. He had demonstrated the ability to develop a product that consumers wanted, and bring it to market. With Cobra's position in the domestic market secure, the breweries contracted, and new products developed, he knew it was time to apply his talent to other territories. So in 2002, Bilimoria had selected three markets for special treatment: India, the US, and South Africa.

Of the three, Bilimoria believed the country with the most potential was his birthplace, India. On the face of it, it didn't seem that encouraging. In the entire seven years that Cobra was brewed in Bangalore, not a single bottle had been sold in the country of production. But by 2002, Bilimoria decided it was time to make inroads into a beer market which was still in its infancy but had massive potential.

CHRIS EDGCUMBE-RENDLE: COBRA'S BUSINESS DEVELOPMENT DIRECTOR

What is your connection with Karan Bilimoria and Cobra Beer?

My connection with Karan started ten years ago, when Cobra Beer was a relatively small, new company. Karan approached me to join his team, as he recognised the need to build a solid distribution base in the UK.

I was first employed in this role, later expanding internationally. My current role is as sales and business development director with responsibility for all non-Indian restaurant sales, new product development and overseeing the subsidiary offices.

What makes Cobra special as a business?

The elements that have contributed to Cobra's success, I feel, are:

1 having a strong leader with clear strategic vision, with a good management team to drive it through.
2 doing things differently, better and changing the marketplace forever.
3 fantastic products.
4 giving employees a sense of belonging to 'the Cobra team'.

What aspect of the Cobra business would you hold up as best practice to other entrepreneurs and business owners?

I would recommend that any entrepreneur take note of Cobra Beer's willingness to take risks – calculated, of course – and never to compromise on the quality of the products.

Could you recall one memory or story of your experiences with Cobra that defines the Karan Bilimoria and Cobra approach to business?

An example that I feel best illustrates Karan's visionary approach would be the King Cobra story. When we decided to research the potential of launching a strong beer, all the focus groups and received wisdom was that the project should be dropped. Most people, even in Cobra, were negative. Karan, however, knew it would work and it has been a great success.

I should note here that I shared his optimism!

When China began its programme of economic liberalisation in 1978, one of the first things to happen was a move to change the nation's drinking culture and promote the sale of beer, rather than the spirit drinking that was the norm. Over the following 25 years, per capita consumption of beer rose from under one litre to 20 litres. In 2003, China overtook the USA as the largest beer market in the world. Bilimoria was well aware of what had happened in China, and he was banking on a similar story in India.

Bilimoria wasn't the only beer magnate with an eye on the main Indian prize. The promise of rich pickings in India had already attracted one major multinational – South African Breweries (SAB) – and other big players in the business, like Interbrew, were waiting in the wings. Then there was India's number one beer brand, Kingfisher, established in 1857, which was gearing up for a fight to keep the top spot, in the face of fierce competition from SAB.

In the circumstances the move into India, as well as the other international markets, required all the entrepreneurship skills that Bilimoria had acquired in building the Cobra Beer business: the attention to detail with the product; working his business network; getting close to the customer; the restless innovation; right down to his instinct for judging the right people to get involved with Cobra brand.

He did have some advantages. Bilimoria's involvement with the Mysore Brewery as Cobra's original brewers, when the company used to import the beer from India, as well as his local contacts, meant that Cobra was better placed than most 'foreign' brands to take on the domestic market. And by now the Indian market was well aware of Cobra beer. Reports of its success had run regularly in the local press and many Indian visitors to London had sampled it and were struck by its quality. By now there was pent-up demand for Cobra in the subcontinent.

Focus groups and formal market research has its place, but Bilimoria likes to take every opportunity to find out what consumers think of Cobra's products. India was no exception. The first consignment of Cobra beer and General Bilimoria wine was sent over to cater for a party thrown by one of Bilimoria's cousins. 'We got excellent feedback at this function,' recalls Bilimoria. 'Everyone loved the wines and the beer, so we got more confident. We decided the time had come to open an office in India.'

Bilimoria knew that succeeding in the Indian market would mean brewing there. Beer made in the West – with all that meant in terms of production cost – was hit with a swathe of import duties and state taxes the moment it reached Indian shores. It was priced out of all but a small segment of the market. Burdened with duties of up to 400 per cent, it could only hope to prosper in a context where the only competition was other imported brands and that meant behind the bars of five-star hotels.

So, once again, Bilimoria began the search for a suitable brewer, this time in India. Although he had maintained a good relationship with the Mysore Brewery, he couldn't return there as it had been bought out by South African Breweries a year earlier, in 2001.

Accompanied by Robert Knox, Bilimoria scoured the country for a suitable producer, going from one brewery to another until they found one run by an offshoot of one of the largest brewing families in India. Situated just inside the Rajasthan border, within easy reach of Delhi, it was run by the Mount Shivalik Group, which has 20 per cent of the beer market in north India and 8 per cent of the national market.

At the time Mount Shivalik's biggest selling brand was a 'super-strong' beer called Thunderbolt, its other main brands were Stroh's, Punjab Extra Strong and Golden Peacock. These were produced in two breweries, one in Rajasthan and the other in Punjab.

Bilimoria felt that people at Mount Shivalik were the right people and was impressed by the brewery's willingness to work with Cobra, even to the extent of upgrading their equipment.

'We liked the people, and they said they were happy to brew for us, even after we told them they needed to modify their plant a lot and their systems,' says Bilimoria. 'We jointly paid for the investment, because it would benefit their products as well. What I liked about their attitude was that they said they were going to learn from us. They weren't resistant to change. So, under the supervision of Robert Knox, we upgraded the whole brewery. Right from the milling stage to the brew house, to the lager stage, to the packaging, we installed new equipment, new systems, and new processes.'

They also managed to recruit a 'super-talented' young Sikh brewmaster called Gurdeep Singh. In all, Bilimoria estimates that Cobra contributed in excess of $1m to the revamp.

By January 2005, Mount Shivalik was producing its first batches of Cobra and it was soon clear that all the time, effort and money that had gone into getting things just right had paid off. The beer was entered for the Monde Selection Awards in Brussels and was rewarded with two gold medals.

In marketing terms, Cobra's launch strategy was to target the four so-called metros – Delhi in the north, Chennai in the south, Kolkata in the east and Mumbai in the west – and a hand-picked selection of other cities and states, including Pune, Rajasthan and Hyderabad, as well as Goa. Bangalore, Uttar Pradesh, Punjab and Haryana were next on the distribution list.

As sales increased in India, the company's infrastructure also expanded. Apart from building up the office in Mumbai, team members were appointed for different cities, and a number of distributors were signed up. In 2006, Cobra India employed around 50 staff, with Bilimoria's cousin Perses Bilimoria heading the team and Poonam Chandel, a drinks industry expert, as vice president, marketing.

Bilimoria is pinning most of his hopes for growth in the Indian market on King Cobra, the company's innovative premium strength offering produced with the Indian market – where strong beer dominates – in mind.

At the end of 2006, within two years of commencing brewing in India, for India, Cobra was being brewed in four locations across the country, with two more breweries in the pipeline and due to begin brewing in 2007. In the six months from March to September 2006, Cobra's sales in India increased by 600 per cent.

ACROSS THE ATLANTIC

As Cobra was making steady progress in India it was also moving into other markets, including the biggest market of them all: the US.

With its huge population of beer drinkers, America was an obvious target. Cobra was launched there in the autumn of 2002. The initial response from the US consumers was very good. The beer made promising inroads into the US market, in the New York curry house market in particular.

However, there were also problems. The American brewing giant Anheuser-Busch produces a malt liquor called King Cobra, and there were fears that the US based company might sue Cobra over trademark infringement. Bilimoria was not taking any chances. He decided to withdraw the product and change its name.

KARAN'S BUSINESS TIPS: EXTERNAL FORCES

No matter how brilliant an entrepreneur is, they will always be subject to unpredictable external forces. Techniques like scenario planning can help a company anticipate possible events in the future. But there is always the risk that something out of the entrepreneur's control will adversely impact on the business.

Bilimoria has made a serious investment in the India market. If predictions are correct, that India's population growth will outpace China's to reach 1.6bn by 2050, making India the world's most populous nation, then Bilimoria may have made a wise investment for the short and long term prosperity of the business he created.

However, Bilimoria is pinning his hopes on the willingness of politicians to introduce economic reforms and promote growth in the beer market. 'When the Indian beer market opens up it may well grow the way the Chinese beer market has grown,' he says. 'It could grow between 25 to 40 times in the next twenty years, from one of the smallest beer markets in the world to one of the biggest.'

But it is not a certainty. An alternative to weaning people off spirits and onto beer is prohibition. Several states have attempted this in the past and Gujarat still bans the sale of alcohol. Bilimoria believes that the net result of the prohibition policy is that the government loses out on the excise duty, the consumer pays more for a product of unpredictable quality and the bootleggers are the only winners.

Bilimoria adds that although India has stumbled on the road of liberalisation that began in 1991, the pace of reform has increased significantly over the past five years, and he believes that it will only increase looking ahead.

'Now the consumer wants reform, and many of the industries and businesses which had once lobbied for protectionism have started beginning to argue for reform. I also realised that the government, regardless of which party was in power in India, was always pro reform, pro liberalisation,' says Bilimoria. 'I knew that when those three constituencies were aligned – consumers, business and government – as being pro liberalisation there would be no turning back. It would only be a question of how quickly could India reform.'

KARAN'S BUSINESS TIPS: MANAGEMENT AND LEADERSHIP

Is there a distinction? The simple distinction is that the management part is the execution part, the delivery part and the leadership part is inspirational, motivational and about taking things forward, Bilimoria says. 'Actually you have got to do both. I think as a chief executive – as an entrepreneur and founder – the visionary strategic element ... that has got to be the most important part.'

After some brainstorming, and with the help of Team Saatchi, Cobra came up with an alternative name: Mogul. After establishing that the name had not been trademarked in the US, and conducting some market research which produced a positive response to the new name, Bilimoria prepared for a launch. Only for disaster to strike again. A belated Google search revealed that a small brewer based in Oregon had been selling a beer called Mogul Madness since 1991 and thus had the rights to the name.

Following the snake theme, Cobra was finally launched early in 2004 in New York, New Jersey and California, this time as Krait – another snake common to India. Krait took a different route to the US consumer than Cobra beer did in the UK. Instead of starting out in Indian restaurants, Krait went straight into the mainstream of pubs, clubs and restaurants of every nationality, where it competes with the likes of Corona, Heineken and Bass.

'We are extremely excited about Krait's entry into the US beer market,' said Bilimoria at the launch. 'This is a significant step in growing worldwide operations and establishing the Cobra brand as a competitive, global beer brand.' Today, the US operation is run by a team of four under the regional director Hoshang Chenoy. Although the branding issue in the USA makes it the most challenging of Cobra's global operations, Bilimoria remains optimistic.

Progress is also being made in South Africa, where Cobra started its subsidiary in Cape Town, headed by Bruce Walker, in June 2003. Like the US, South Africa has a large beer market, and while South African Breweries had a market share of around 98 per cent it was felt that the consumers were crying out for more choice. SAB's brand Castle currently dominates the market and only a handful of international brands have moved in. Cobra's sales in South Africa have been building extremely well, and the brand has excellent exposure in Cape Town, with expansion in Johannesburg underway. If Cobra manages to gain just one or two per cent of the market, that would represent a sizeable volume.

Meanwhile, Cobra is yet to crack the biggest market of all. 'We looked at China,' says Bilimoria, 'I went with Tony Blair on a delegation to China and India in 2005, and the potential there is so clear. In China, however, we would definitely have to brew locally, because the cost of production is so low it is not competitive to export there.'

A COBRA FUTURE

Cobra's future looks bright. The introduction of new products such as Cobra 0.0%, Lower Carb and King Cobra came alongside a comprehensive extension to the formats in which Cobra drinks were made available. In December 2003, the company had three SKUs – stock-keeping units – the big bottle, the small bottle and the draught version in kegs. But, within three years, that total had risen to 30. Suddenly, it was possible to order every variety of Cobra, not only in bottles but in small cans or big cans, singly or in four-packs.

Apart from growth in Cobra's home market, Bilimoria is keen to build on the company's forays abroad. The brand is now exported to over 45 countries around the world and has opened offices in three foreign territories: India, South Africa and the US.

Bilimoria sees huge potential for sales growth in developing countries. While per capita consumption of beer is 165 litres in the Czech Republic and 99 litres in the UK, in South Africa the equivalent figure is 65 litres, in China 20 litres. The lesson of regions such as the former Soviet bloc, where vodka consumption was rife, is that once governments make concerted attempts to wean their populations off spirits and onto beer, growth rates can be staggering.

'In Russia in the nineties, they decided they'd rather people drank beer than vodka,' says Bilimoria. 'They opened up beer production in Russia and, as a result, its beer market has been one of the fastest growing beer markets in the world for the last 15 years. In Poland the same thing is happening. The Polish beer market has rocketed.'

India will undoubtedly be a hard market to crack but it is likely to be the market that defines Cobra as a company. A visit to the Hotel Gokul in Mumbai tells you everything you need to know about the maturity of the beer market there. The Gokul is a stereotypical working man's bar, which serves a wide selection of drinks and snacks such as tandoori chicken, with curry sauce, roti, and wedges of lemon, as wall-mounted fans fight a losing battle against the midday heat.

On a late Saturday lunchtime in March 2006, it was about a third full. But look around you on the formica-topped tables and there is not a bottle of beer in sight. In a country where the average drinker bases alcohol purchasing decisions on the amount of kick for the buck, spirits are the thing. So the choice on offer ranges from locally-bottled Smirnoff and Bacardi, to the euphemistically named 'country liquor'. This last tipple is a sort of bathtub gin made in the back yard which should come with a health warning as such concoctions have been the cause of many deaths over the years (up to 50 per cent of the alcohol drunk in India today is said to be country liquor).

The big winner in the official spirits market is whisky. At the Gokul, for example, around a dozen whisky brands are listed, including domestic names such as St Paul's and Imperial. The only solace for the beer producer at this particular bar is that on two tables, there is a Tupperware jug of lager alongside the quarter bottle of whisky and a bottle of water.

It is no surprise to hear then that, while British consumption of beer per capita is 99 litres per year, in India the equivalent figure is 0.67 litres, supporting a market of just under 100 million cases annually. This in a country of 1.1 billion people.

Apart from the dominance of spirits, another problem facing alcohol producers is that India's highly federalised system of government not only leaves each of the 35 State and Union Territory authorities with the power to charge their own excise duties and taxes on beer produced by in-state breweries, but also the right to impose an additional tariff on product imported from other states in the union. As a result, the customer can end up paying four or five times the ex-brewery cost for his bottle of beer. In purchasing power parity terms, beer is still an unaffordable luxury for the majority of Indians.

As if all that weren't enough, there is a cultural battle to be fought too. In India, drinking remains something of a guilty pleasure. It is also frowned upon for women to touch alcohol, though this taboo is being broken down among the younger generation. And while one beer executive estimates that 98 per cent of Indian men drink, many will avoid doing so in front of their parents or grandparents. But things are changing. And fast. Beer sales are growing at eight per cent a year and, if the lesson of China is anything to go by, India could become an extremely lucrative market in a relatively short space of time.

In the short term Cobra cannot hope to match the production capacity or marketing might of the likes of UB and SAB. Between them they have taken to brewing in nearly every state in a bid not only to save on duties and thus drive prices down, but to cut freight costs which can be considerable in a country the size of India.

But while Cobra may be in no position to topple the big two in the short term at least, it does have ambitious plans. As ever, it is impossible not to be persuaded by Bilimoria's enthusiasm and optimism. It is a glimpse of the qualities that have taken this irrepressible entrepreneur to the top flight of the UK beer business, and possibly soon to become one of the world's major players in the sector.

'It is only a matter of time before it happens in India,' says Bilimoria. 'I am not saying that we are ever going to get near the level of the Czech Republic, but the Indian beer market can certainly get to South African standards, in which case you are talking 100 times the beer market that it is today. And that could very well happen. So we've built up huge, huge confidence and faith that India is going to be our biggest market looking ahead.'

And you would not bet against Bilimoria and Cobra succeeding, as the company heads towards a flotation sometime in 2008 or 2009. 'Stella Artois was founded in the 14th century,' notes Bilimoria. 'Cobra Beer was founded just over 14 years ago. When we started Cobra, we were up against giants in an industry which is centuries old. The Cobra story itself is a great example of what can be done with innovation.

KARAN'S BUSINESS TIPS:
VISION, MISSION

Many, many big companies confuse their mission with their vision. The mission is the '*What?*' ... you can measure it. So, in our case, to brew the finest ever Indian beer and make it a global beer brand. But more importantly I believe – equally important if not more important than the mission, is the vision.

The vision is the '*Why?*'. The vision is what underlies everything that you do, it is what you live and breathe by, it is your attitude, it is your state of mind.

And it's our vision. Aspire – where do you want your business to get to? Achieve – how are you going to get there? And so we had 'to aspire and achieve against all odds with integrity'.

And the good thing about it is that it is almost a definition of entrepreneurship. You come up with an idea, you want to get somewhere with an idea, invariably you have got limited means, invariably you have got all the odds stacked against you and then you go out and you make it happen. And the best thing about being in business, the best thing about being an entrepreneur, is the opportunities are endless. And the sky literally is the limit. And it is great fun.

'Why did it take a student to come up with an idea of producing a less gassy, smooth lager that accompanies food and appeals to ale drinkers? Why is it that it has taken a British brand of Indian origin to brew a beer in Poland and Belgium and create the world's first double fermented lager? That is the power of innovation, that's the sort of entrepreneurial spirit and innovative creativity that sets us apart, and enables us to compete as a David against Goliath.'

'There is only one way to learn,' the alchemist answered. 'It's through action. Everything you need to know you have learned through your journey.'

From *The Alchemist* by Paulo Coelho

KARAN'S TEN TOP TIPS FOR GROWTH

1 Have a mission. Research and understand your market thoroughly.
2 Be different. Be better. Change the marketplace forever.
3 Take the lead and do not follow.
4 Be innovative and creative.
5 Look always to the future and take a long-term view.
6 Be passionate and proud of your product.
7 It requires focus, commitment, drive, hard work, sacrifice. And never giving up.
8 Build a great team and invest in your people.
9 Balance growth with responsibility and be outward looking.
10 Aspire and achieve against all odds, with integrity. The sky is the limit.

COBRA AWARDS

Monde Selection, Brussels – World Selection of Quality Awards

2006 – 1 Grand Gold Medal and 11 Gold Medals – the most in the world for beer

2006 – 3 International High Quality Trophies

2005 – 2 Grand Gold Medals and 9 Gold Medals – the most in the world for beer

2004 – 2 Grand Gold Medals and 4 Gold Medals

2003 – International High Quality Trophy

2003, 2002, 2001 – Gold Medal

CoolBrand 2005, 2006

Awarded by Superbrands

International Beer Challenge 2006 – 7th place, World's 50 Best Beers – King Cobra

World Beer Cup 2006 – Bronze Medal, American-Style Low-Carbohydrate Light Lager – Cobra Lower Cal Lower Carb

Drinks Business Awards 2006

Winner, Man of the Year – Karan Bilimoria CBE DL, founder and chief executive, Cobra Beer

Winner, Business Excellence – Cobra Beer

Runner-up, Consumer Campaign – Cobra Beer for CobraVision

Runner-up, Best Design and Packaging – King Cobra

CLASS Drink Packaging Design Awards 2006

Best Beer – Cobra Premium 5%

Highly Commended – King Cobra

Ranked in the *Europe's 500* Awards list, 2005, 2006

Diversity within a Private Sector Organisation – Awarded at MACE 2005 (Multicultural Awards on Competitiveness and Enterprise)

The Drinks Business Awards 2005
Business Excellence Award

***Sunday Times* annual listing of the UK's Best Companies to Work For**
Top 100 SMEs to Work For in the UK 2005, 2006
Top 50 SMEs to Work For in the UK 2004
Top 25 SMEs to Work For in London 2005

Best Companies Ltd
Ranked 8th best SME to Work For in London

Investors in People (IIP) 2004
Presented by Ruth Spellman, President of IIP
2004 GRAMIA Award

The Grocery Advertising and Marketing Industry (GRAMIA) Awards
Beer Design of the Year Award
Wine & Spirit International, Design Awards 2004
Gold Medal
Wine & Spirit International, Design Awards 2004
Innovation Award, September 2003
Packaging News
Business of the Year 2003

Asian Business Awards
2002 – The Grocery Advertising and Marketing Industry Awards (GRAMIA) Award
Virgin Atlantic Fast Track 100
1999 – League table of Britain's fastest growing unquoted companies

International Food and Beverage Creative Excellence Awards (FAB awards)
2001 & 2002 FAB award for the best poster in the alcoholic drinks category
1999 FABULOUS Award for Best Press Campaign overall
1999 FAB Award for Best Press Campaign for Alcoholic Drinks

The Arts & Business Awards
1999 'Arts & Business Scotland' pairing award 'Cobra Beer and the Edinburgh Mela'

KARAN BILIMORIA – AWARDS

Special Recognition Award, UKTI India Business Awards, 2006
Honorary Doctor of the University, Staffordshire University, 2006
Man of the Year, Drinks Business Awards, 2006
Honorary Doctor of Letters, Heriot-Watt University, 2005
Indo British Partnership Award, Non-Resident Indian (NRI) Institute, 2005
Honorary Doctor of Business, Brunel University, 2005
Outstanding Achievement Award, Institute of Chartered Accountants in England and Wales, 2005
Business Person of the Year, London Chamber of Commerce and Industry, 2004
Albert Medal, Royal Society for the Encouragement of Arts, Manufactures and Commerce, 2004
Commander of the Order of the British Empire, Her Majesty The Queen's Birthday Honours List, 2004
Best Business Leader (25 –100 employees), Sage Business Awards, 2004
Entrepreneur of the Year, London and South East of England, National Business Awards, 2004
Pride of India Award, Non-Resident Indian (NRI) Institute, 2004
Excellence Award, NRI Institute, 2003
Entrepreneur of the Year, London Chamber of Commerce and Industry, 2003
Entrepreneur of the Year, Asian Achievers Awards, 2003
London Entrepreneur of the Year (Consumer Products), Ernst & Young, 2003
Asian of the Year, 2002
Outstanding Achievement Award, Executives Association of Great Britain, 2002
NRI Millennium Honour, 2001

KARAN BILIMORIA – APPOINTMENTS AND MEMBERSHIPS:

Appointed The Lord Bilimoria, of Chelsea, June 2006

Representative Deputy Lieutenant, London Borough of Hounslow, 2005 –

Deputy Lieutenant, Greater London, 2001 –

UK Chairman, Indo British Partnership, 2003 –

Chairman, Indo British Partnership Network (IBPN), 2005 –

Member, UK-India Round Table, 2005 –

Member, Asia Task Force, 2005 –

Member, National Employment Panel, Department for Work and Pensions, 2001 –

Chairman, SME (Small and Medium Size Enterprise) Board, National Employment Panel, 2001–2005

Member, New Deal Task Force, Department for Education and Employment, 1999–2001

Member, The Neighbourhood Renewal Private Sector Panel, Office of the Deputy Prime Minister, 2003–2005

Chancellor, Thames Valley University, 2005 –

Governor, Thames Valley University, 2001–2004

Vice Chairman, Asian Business Association, London Chamber of Commerce and Industry, 2003 –

National Champion, National Council for Graduate Entrepreneurship, 2004

Visiting Entrepreneur, Centre for Entrepreneurial Learning, University of Cambridge, 2004 –

Champion, Make Your Mark campaign, Enterprise Insight, 2005 –

Honorary Life Fellow, Royal Society for the Encouragement of Arts, Manufactures and Commerce (FRSA), 2004 –

Member, Council, Royal Society for the Encouragement of Arts, Manufactures and Commerce, 2004 –

Patron, Royal Society for the Encouragement of Arts, Manufactures and Commerce, India, 2005 –

Member, Development Board, Royal Society for the Encouragement of Arts, Manufactures and Commerce, 2005 –

Member, Young Presidents' Organization (YPO), London, 2000 –

Chairman, Young Presidents' Organization (YPO), London, 2004–2005

Member, Young Presidents' Organization (YPO) International Education Committee, 2003–2005

Member, HRH The Duke of York's Council

Charter Member, The Indus Entrepreneurs (TiE) UK, 2002 –
Board Member, The Indus Entrepreneurs (TiE) UK, 2003 –
Member, President's Committee, London First, 2002–2006
Member, London Business School Foundation for Entrepreneurial Management, Enterprise 100, 1999 –
Member, Advisory Council, CIDA Foundation UK, 2006 –
Member, Drapers' Company, 2005 –
Freeman, Freedom of the City of London in The Company of Drapers, 2005 –
Companion, Chartered Management Institute, 2005 –
Founding President, UK Zoroastrian Chamber of Commerce, 2003–2006
Honorary President, Training for Life, 2004 –
Member, UK India Consultative Group, Foreign & Commonwealth Office, 2002–2003
Mentor, Metropolitan Police Joint Mentoring Initiative, 2002–2004
Governor, The Ditchley Foundation, 2004 –
Member, The Tyson Task Force on the Recruitment and Development of Non–Executive Directors, 2003
Member, Bank of England – LCCI/Asian Business Association Panel, 2000 –
Chairman, Memorial Gates Committee, 2003 –
Vice Patron, Memorial Gates Trust, 1999–2004
Trustee, British Cardiovascular Research Trust, 2006 –
Ambassador, Interactive University UK, 2005 –
Member, Birmingham Business School Advisory Board, 2005 –
Patron, Thare Machi Starfish Initiative, 2001 –
Patron, Rethink severe mental illness, 2003 –
Patron, India International Foundation
Champion, Roko Cancer Appeal (MKC Trust), 2005 –
Chairman, Advisory Board, Shrimati Pushpa Wati Loomba Memorial Trust, 2001 –
Patron, Thames Community Foundation, 2005 –
Patron, St Andrew's University Cricket Club, 2001 –
Fellow, Institute of Directors, 2005 –
Honorary Member, Cranfield Management Association, 2005 –
International Envoy, London, 2005
Ambassador, London 2012 Olympic Bid, 2005
Founding Patron, Oxford Entrepreneurs, 2004 –
Vice President, Cambridge Union, 1988
Member, Cambridge University Polo Team (Half Blue Awarded), 1988

KARAN BILIMORIA'S DESERT ISLAND DISCS (BROADCAST SUNDAY 13 JUNE, 2004)

1 Nessun Dorma – Luciano Pavarotti, Placido Domingo, Jose Carreras
2 Soul – Shayan
3 Amazing Grace – Bands and pipes of the Household Division
4 (I can't get no) Satisfaction – The Rolling Stones
5 Samba Pa Ti – Santana
6 Symphony for Organ Op 42 No 5 – Ian Tracey and BBC Philharmonic Orchestra; Composer, Charles-Marie Widor
7 What a Wonderful World – Louis Armstrong
8 Raga – Ravi Shankar

Favourite record: What a Wonderful World
Book: Instead of the Bible, *The Gathas of Zarathushtra*, and *The Alchemist* by Paulo Coelho
Luxury: *Yes Minister* and *Yes Prime Minister* videos

TIMELINE

COBRA AND KARAN BILIMORIA (KB): A TIMELINE

1961   (26 November) Karan Bilimoria born.

1981   KB graduates in Commerce from Indian Institute of Management & Commerce, Osmania University, Hyderabad, India.

       KB travels to England to study accountancy.

1982   KB joins accountants Arthur Young (later Ernst & Young).

1986   KB qualifies as a chartered accountant and leaves accountants Arthur Young; then goes up to Cambridge to study law.

1988   KB graduates from Cambridge and starts as accountant with Cresvale.

1989   KB leaves Cresvale and starts in business.

       (February) Founds A&K International with Arjun Reddy.

       KB starts developing Cobra Beer before going to Bangalore.

       Business run on overdraft and government backed loan.

1990   (February) KB goes to India.

       Name changed from Panther to Cobra.

       (End of April) First beer imported to UK.

       Cobra Beer headquarters move from Fulham to King's Road, Chelsea.

       Supplies free beer for Channel 4 party.

       Iqbal Wahhab becomes Cobra's public relations advisor.

       (December) Stabilises the taste of the beer.

1991   Reaching 100 restaurants – 1000 cases of 660ml per month.

       Gandhi deal provides £100,000.

1992   Sponsors *Good Curry Guide*.

1993   Samson Sohail joins.

       Grant Thornton suggests raising £250,000.

       (October) Pierre Brahm invests £50,000 as angel investor for 5%.

	(December) £190,000 raised through balance of government backed loan scheme. Cobra valued at £1 million.
1994	(September) Starts *Tandoori* magazine.
1995	Arjun Reddy leaves the business.
	Fundraising – ordinary and preference shares. Cobra valued at £1.5 million. KB's share diluted down to 72%.
1996	Christopher Edgcumbe-Rendle joins
	(autumn) KB meets Jim Robertson, head brewer and production director Charles Wells. Brewing moved to UK.
1997	Brewing starts in UK.
	Team Saatchi hired for advertising.
1998	Simon Edwards joins as marketing/sales director.
	HQ moved to Coda Centre on Munster Road, Fulham.
	Curryholic Dave is born.
	KB attends Business Growth Programme at Cranfield School of Management.
	(February) *Tandoori* magazine runs article that prompts boycott of Cobra. Tough cost-cutting ensues.
1999	(March) Boycott officially withdrawn.
	(November) General Bilimoria Wines launched.
	Cobra listed in Fast Track 100 list of the UK's fastest growing companies.
2001	HQ moved to Peterborough Road, Parsons Green, London.
	KB decides to broaden production base.
	Dynshaw Italia joins as finance director.
	Enters Monde Selection, Brussels, World Selection of Quality Awards and wins Gold Medal.
2002	(March) Office opened in Mumbai, India.
	(autumn) Cobra expands to US with an office in New York City.
	(October) Hires SHS Sales and Marketing.
	Christopher Edgcumbe-Rendle leaves.

2003   First TV commercials.

(March) First national TV advertising campaign.

(May) KB Travels to Kielce, Poland to check out brewery, Browar Belgia.

(June) Cobra launched in South Africa with an office in Cape Town.

(July) Embossed icons introduced on bottles.

Chris Edgcumbe-Rendle returns.

The Grand Canyon plan.

2004   (June) Exports Krait to US.

2005   (January) Mount Shivalik brewery in India produces first Cobra beer.

(January) Launch of CobraVision.

(January) Cobra 0.0%; brewing commenced in the Netherlands.

(May) Cobra Lower Cal.

2006   Off-trade sales function comes back in-house from SHS.

(February) King Cobra, the world's first double-fermented lager; brewing commenced in Belgium.

(March) Cobra Foundation launched.

Medal haul at 2006 Monde Selection World Quality Awards: Grand Gold Medal; Gold Medal (11); Silver Medal (5) – more than any other beer in the world for the second year running.

INDEX

WITHDRAWN
FROM STOCK
QMUL LIBRARY

WILEY

Also available from Capstone

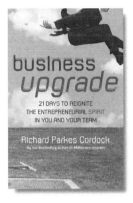

ISBN 9/8184112/446

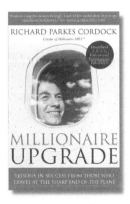

ISBN 9/8184112/033

ISBN 9781841126807

ISBN 9781841126869

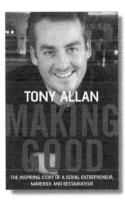

ISBN 9781841126319

ISBN 9781841127019

CAPSTONE
be inspired!

QM LIBRARY
(MILE END)